# THE SECRET
# BETWEEN US

## Competition Among Women

## LAURA TRACY

LITTLE, BROWN AND COMPANY

*Boston   Toronto   London*

*First Edition*

The names of people in this book and some identifying details have been changed for reasons of privacy.

"You Fit Into Me" from *Power Politics* by Margaret Atwood. Copyright © Margaret Atwood, 1971, House of Anansi Press. Reprinted by permission of Stoddart Publishing Co., Limited, 34 Lesmill Rd., Don Mills, Ontario, Canada.

*Library of Congress Cataloging-in-Publication Data*

Tracy, Laura, 1947–
    The secret between us : competition among women / Laura Tracy. — 1st ed.
        p.    cm.
    Includes bibliographical references and index.
    ISBN 0-316-85220-1
    1. Women — Psychology.  2. Competition (Psychology).  I. Title.
HQ1206.T73   1991
305.42 — dc20
                            90-49498

10  9  8  7  6  5  4  3  2  1

RRD-VA

Published simultaneously in Canada by Little, Brown & Company (Canada) Limited

*Printed in the United States of America*

ALSO BY LAURA TRACY

*Catching the Drift:*
Authority, Gender, and Narrative Strategy in Fiction

# The Secret Between Us

*For Aaron, Jessie, Doug, and Florence*

# Contents

# Acknowledgments

Many, many women and men contributed to the making of this book. In particular, I am enormously grateful to Florence Roisman, Gail Harmon, Elizabeth Velez, Michele Orwin, Lorna Irvine, and Douglas LaBier for their continuous and loving support and their insistence on asking the hard questions. Special thanks to my mother, Anne Kaplan, my sister, Judith Cahan, and my daughter, Jessie Tracy, who agreed to make what I hope are loving appearances in several chapters. Long conversations with Michael Pertschuk, Robert Stein, Ken Josniak, Michael Daniels, and Kermit Moyer about men and competition made it possible for me to understand the "other" side. My editor, Patricia Mulcahy, and her assistant, Christine Archibald, provided invaluable editorial assistance and generous encouragement. Without my agent, Eric Ashworth, this book would not have been written.

Much to my regret, I am unable to thank by name so many of the women with whom I talked since they requested anonymity. You know who you are and, I hope, how grateful I am to you.

# *Preface*

Competition between and among women has interested me for many years. Teaching literature, I long ago realized that all the books I read and loved got somehow to the subject of competition between women very quickly. From Jane Austen to Fay Weldon and Grace Paley, the writers I taught in courses on gender and narrative all focused on the way women relate to each other and, therefore, on competition. For me, the issue was how to understand competition as more than malice and backbiting, how to reconcile the loving portraits of female characters contained in the books I read with the terrible acts those characters performed on each other.

In part, *The Secret Between Us* grows out of that question. But my own personal experiences with women competing against each other were equally important. Before writing this book, I firmly believed—like every other woman I interviewed—that I did not compete with other women, both as a point of principle and a matter of desire. As a feminist, I wanted to believe that women could be more supportive than competitive, that we wanted to connect with each other far more than we wanted to hurt each other.

Not too long ago, I discovered otherwise. Living through a painful experience with professional competition made me begin to think about the real relationships women forge, the ones we have learned *not* to talk about in this postfeminist era. And, thinking about that experience as someone used to analyzing writers in relation to the stories they tell, I realized that my research would have to start with an examination of my own participation in the competition, which was so hurtful and unexpected.

I discovered that I had been both right and wrong. Most women *do* want to connect with each other, most of the time. But many, just as I had done, convince themselves that the competition they despise is another woman's fault. Instead of actors, we think of ourselves as victims, not responsible for the sometimes terrible relationships between women we endure, and at the mercy of the "other" women who lack the scruples or moral sense we possess.

I also discovered something else: that competition *is* the tie that binds women together in our patriarchal society. When most of us compete, we act out a distorted version of our fundamental desire to connect, whether we are mothers and daughters, sisters, friends, professional rivals, or jousters for a man. At some point in our conversations, all the women I interviewed recognized an awful fact—that each spent much, much more time and energy thinking about her competitor than about the people she loved.

Despite the fact that women display an intense interest in their competitors, none of the hundreds of books discussing women's lives addresses directly the topic of competition between women. Right now, competition between women is a taboo subject, much as adultery was only thirty or so years ago. Then, trying to make sense of her experience with an extramarital affair, one of my friends was able to find the subject explicitly discussed only in *Anna Karenina* and *Madame Bovary*, books written by men. Now, after searching for a book containing some advice and consolation about the competition wreaking havoc in my own life, I realized that if I wanted to read it, I would have to write it.

During the two years I spent researching and writing this book, talking to approximately one hundred women between the ages of fifteen and seventy-five, I learned that the taboo silencing us is the same dynamic that keeps us apart. I learned that only when we recognize our own competitiveness can we change the way we relate to each other. And I came to understand that most women deeply desire to make such a change, to alter and repair the sorts of relationships that make us fear each other and despise ourselves.

Learning *not* to compete is the wrong answer for most of us. Instead, understanding that the desperation we feel when we *do* compete is a response to a deeper feeling of disconnection can allow us to choose our competitions, and how we want to behave when we're in them.

*The Secret Between Us* is not a "how-to" book. It is a book that opens for discussion a subject that's very painful and controversial for most women. It is a book, I hope, that will provoke conversations that make women stronger, both individually and with each other.

L.T.

*The Secret Between Us*

# Chapter

# 1

# *Telling the Secret*

## A CONSPIRACY OF SILENCE

"I never compete with other women. I'm just not a competitive person."

"It makes me feel sick. I'll do anything to avoid competing with another woman."

"It's a real problem. Other women are so competitive. I'm not, but sometimes I don't know how to handle their hostility. I hate the indirectness and the manipulation."

"Women can be so mean. I've had much worse experiences with women competing than with men. Women always know your weak spots, and they don't hesitate to zero in. I know I never do that."

"You're writing a book about competition between women? Boy, can I tell you some stories! Women are really vicious."

*   *   *

3

In a certain way, this book is about a conspiracy of silence among women, one that conceals the secret we hate to tell—that of our own competitiveness.

As women talked to me about competition, the interviews, more often than not, felt like cloak-and-dagger sessions. Their voices dropped as they leaned toward me, speaking off the record. They seemed ashamed of acknowledging female competition, and inevitably, as they talked, they told stories, one after the other, about *other women competing with them*—stories filled with treachery, duplicity, malice, and flat-out craziness. No one mentioned her own competitiveness. According to the research material I collected, and in terms of my own feelings about women's competition *before* I began this book, only *other* women compete.

Clearly, something is wrong here.

Especially today, when the feminist movement calls on women to bond in sisterhood, talking about women and competition feels like a general betrayal of all women. Talking about women competing is telling other women's secrets.

Yet whether we like it or not, we live in a competitive society. Our economy is competitive by design, and as a nation, we see in competition a challenge to develop our resources and ourselves.

But women have been taught that competition is unethical, even immoral. We've been socialized against full participation in our economy and our history. We've been taught to be *secret* competitors, and our secret has kept us subordinate members of our society. Most of us recognize competition only when it's practiced by another woman. Even worse, many of us often don't realize we are *in* a competition until we've lost it.

Telling the secret of women's competition is telling the secret of women's desires and women's fears. Like men, we compete to get what we want. But unlike men, often we are afraid we want too much. Even more often, we confuse wanting with selfishness.

Anne, twenty-two, feels selfish most of the time. Nearly six feet tall, with long brown hair and large hazel eyes, Anne is an arresting figure. Her body language, however, denies both her beauty and her outstanding achievements in school.

Sitting with her shoulders carefully bent forward, her hands neatly crossed in her lap, and her legs wound around each other, Anne physically underlines her belief: "I don't want anything so much that I would compete with another woman to get it."

Anne's body language expresses fear. Wanting makes her feel frightened, and her fear affects her self-esteem. Although she earned excellent grades in college, she feels: "Anyone could have done as well. I work so hard because I know I'm really not very smart."

Anne doesn't want to know how competitive she is. She doesn't want to recognize that the drive and ambition motivating her to achieve make her a competitive winner. As long as she can convince herself that she doesn't want anything badly enough to compete with another woman to get it, she doesn't have to face her own desires.

Anne thinks, as do many women, that if she competes with other women she will be abandoned. Her fears of loneliness and isolation, of being thought by other women to be self-absorbed and selfish, overwhelm her desires.

Most of us share her fear. Sally, twenty, is another brilliant student; she took her name out of a scholarship competition she was sure to win, because her best friend was up for the same award.

Sally believed their friendship would not survive her victory, but she didn't expect her friend to quit the contest. Instead, Sally was convinced that only *she* could absorb her friend's victory.

Like Sally, many of us believe that competition disrupts the ties that bind us together. Yet, when she quit the scholarship contest, Sally demonstrated that the basis of women's relationships with each other is distrust. Sally didn't trust her friend enough to hope that the two of them could, together, face a competition they had not set up. She believed that only she was strong enough to put their relationship before her desire to win, that her friend would leave her if Sally won. She believed that being strong meant sacrificing herself.

Sally and Anne practice the secret competition of the "good girl." Good girls don't compete with each other. They wait to be asked, try not to harm each other, and give up what they want for the good of someone else. But good girls live with a constant dilemma because they are not only good—they're feminine. By now, nearly twenty years into this third wave of the feminist movement, most of us realize the dangers of femininity—that it restricts us, dictating the way we dress, act, talk, and even think. But we often ignore the fact that femininity also controls the way women relate to each other.

When mothers teach their daughters to be feminine, they teach them to distrust and contrast themselves to other women, starting with the mother who is doing the teaching.

Femininity fundamentally pits women against each other. Femininity separates women from each other.

So feminine good girls, like Sally and Anne, keep their competitiveness very secret, especially from themselves. Femininity means innocence. It means keeping the secret that most women know very well, the secret that our relationships with each other are about power, not about community.

When the women I interviewed told me they did not compete with other women, like Sally and Anne they tacitly accepted as a law of female nature the bloody, ruthless, manipulative behaviors traditionally marking competition between women. They made a crucial mistake about female relationships.

The real secret in our society is that the competition between women is the tie that binds us most closely together. After some soul-searching and self-examination, most of the women with whom I talked admitted that, ironically, their most intense and highly charged relationships existed in the context of competition—with mothers-in-law, with rivals for love and business, with their own mothers, daughters, sisters, and friends.

But it is a connection that must be kept secret, especially from ourselves. While keeping us separate from each other is crucial to social definitions of femininity, it is equally important that we don't know it. It is critical that we fail to realize that so much of our intense emotional life is diverted from a connection that could enhance and make us stronger to one that dissipates our energy and fragments our sense of self.

When we agree to keep our competition secret, to carry it out only in private life along personal lines, it becomes a significant force distorting our lives. It becomes the dynamic we deny longest and despair of most. It is what we fear in other women and are ashamed of in ourselves.

We are controlled by our failure to examine our competitiveness with other women, in ways that can make us unconsciously betray deeply held principles and hurt beloved daughters, mothers, sisters, and friends.

Again and again, the women I interviewed repeated that competition with other women made them "feel sick." When we compete with each other, we feel "awful." And we are right to feel that way. We are right because, competing with each other, we act out a relationship of profound distortion. We take our desire to connect with each other and color it with anger, hostility, and shame. We allow ourselves to connect in ways that hurt ourselves and each other.

In our society, the rhetoric of independent development has been aimed at men. Women, in contrast, have been encouraged to develop themselves in relation to the other people in their lives. The self we have been taught to own and to value is a self connected to, not separated from, other people.*

And we are unable to ignore, deny, or rationalize away this identity simply because it's time to compete.

---

* Many contemporary sociologists and psychologists working in the area of women's development believe that women form their identities in connection with the other people in their environment. In particular, see Nancy Chodorow's *The Reproduction of Mothering*, Jean Baker Miller's *Toward a New Psychology of Women*, and Carol Gilligan's *In a Different Voice* and *Mapping the Moral Domain*.

## THE SECRET IS OUT

However, things are changing for women in our society. We can no longer keep our competition—and our desires, ambitions, and fears—secret. The growing number of women in the workplace means that we are forced to experience *open* competition with each other. Right now, that competition is constructed on a masculine model.

Talking to men about competition is a vastly different experience from talking to women about the same subject. The men I interviewed approached the topic with eagerness and thoughtful reflection. Instead of feeling ashamed and humiliated, the men were straightforward, unembarrassed, and unafraid.

Stephen, fifty-seven, a prominent Washington, D.C., lobbyist and advocate, is a good example. As we talked, we ate lunch in a restaurant near his office. We had a "civilized" conversation. In contrast, even the most successful woman I met talked to me in her office, behind closed doors. Chewing, swallowing, managing the silverware and the water glasses—all unthinkable.

Like Stephen, men discuss competition calmly. Their hands don't tremble. Their excitement rises only when they discuss *women's* competition. Their own competitiveness is a matter of course. They know the rules.

Yet talking to men—nice, kind, even sweet, men—I gradually realized that a real gap existed. Although they spoke in rational, measured voices, their words told stories about annihilation, misery, and ruthless determination. They talked, as Stephen said, about "warfare without anger."

For men, "warfare without anger" is competition— open, impersonal, according to a set of rules and a code of

ethics women have never learned. While connection is
the rule for women—connection between people and between the mind and the emotions—separation is the rule
for men.

Traditionally, we think about competition between
men as a challenge. We're not supposed to take personally the destruction it wreaks. Instead, we're supposed to
think of competitive victories as triumphs enhancing self-
development and promoting independence, and competitive losses as defeats leading to dependence.

But when the social psychologist Carol Gilligan listened
to women talk about the lives they really lived, she heard a
"different voice." She heard women say that *their* independence did not include the fortress of invisible women—
mothers, wives, secretaries, daughters, and lovers—who
surround "independent" men. To these women, being independent meant being alone.

Gilligan heard women declare that what they desired
was *interdependence*. She understood that what looks like
women losing competitions really can be women trying not
to win a competition that leaves them alone and lonely.

Unlike men, women develop an "ethic of care" rather
than an "ethic of justice," because women are mothered by
other women. As indicated by Nancy Chodorow, a psychoanalyst, while men are encouraged to separate from their
mothers and identify with their fathers, women base their
identity on remaining attached to their mothers. Hence,
women develop a fluid sense of self, where the boundary
between self and other is less well marked, and far more
permeable, than it is for men. So women "feel" more for
other people than men do. They care about mitigating
circumstances. They get more involved emotionally.

Traditionally, this involvement has caused women a lot

of trouble. Women have been viewed as "soft," vulnerable, and too sensitive to compete with the "hard-nosed maturity" that men display. "Warfare without anger" does not exist for women. We get too angry, too involved, too desperate, and too hurt. Unlike men, we can't ignore our deep feeling that action is successful *only* when it enhances and strengthens relationships.

But what most of us don't realize is that the new open competition between us, which makes us feel so "awful," can provoke real social and personal change. The professional workplace is not the only location where competition between women is no longer a secret. Right now, our family lives, our romances, and our relationships with our friends are all in transition. Open competition among us in every arena of our lives can transform our society.

### OPEN, PERSONAL COMPETITION – CHANGING OURSELVES, CHANGING OUR SOCIETY

When we keep our intellect and our emotions separate, we use psychological denial to maintain the status quo. We resist real change. We say we want it, but unconsciously, we keep ourselves feeling comfortable enough to keep things the same.

Women are no longer comfortable. Forced to compete with each other openly, we are increasingly *un*comfortable. Right now, open competition between women exists precisely at the point of a social lag—a fissure about to crack open traditional assumptions about who women are and what we want.

As long as women competed in secret, only in our private lives, our competition was the glue that kept the patriarchy together by keeping women separate from each other. Historically, open, impersonal competition made men feel good—comfortably masculine—while secret, personal competition made women feel bad—but comfortably feminine.

But now the secret competition practiced according to the rules of femininity is dynamite. Yet open competition is not the same for women as for men. When women compete openly, we retain the personal component of our former secret competitions. We are not able to divorce our emotions. Even though the workplace gives us the right to compete, we still feel wrong when we do so.

Open, *personal* competition allows us to see that the impersonal ethics of marketplace competition are the ethics of the jungle. Competing personally, we can't evade the emotional knowledge that the jungle we live in is one we agree to create.

At the same time, this realization forces us to admit that the old secrecy governing women's relationships existed to conceal the jungle ethics women lived with every day, with each other. We realize that women have never trusted each other, nor were we supposed to. And although now we're told that we should bond with each other, we are not told how to maintain our bonds *while* we compete.

Now that competition between women is out in the open, we can acknowledge that the motivation we feel to connect with each other is strikingly at odds with the impersonal competition that men have always practiced, as well as with our own secret, personal competitions. We can *choose* to compete in ways that affirm instead of destroy our connection with each other.

Eleanor, thirty-nine, is a partner in a corporate law firm in San Francisco. After we talked, she began to think about competition in a new way, about how *she* could change the workplace competition with her female colleagues that seemed to be an unavoidable and terrible feature of her job.

"A management position opened in the firm," Eleanor reported back to me. "It was the first time this kind of job had ever been open to women. One of my female colleagues told me she was going to try for it, and solicited my support. I was in a real quandary, because it was a position I wanted also. I think that before I thought about my own competitiveness I would have tried to avoid telling her that. I would have gone about getting the job secretly, hoping that she would screw up, maybe even making indirect comments about her. This time, I'm proud to say, I decided to tell her that I would not be able to support her because I wanted the job too. What a surprise! We were competing, but neither of us did anything backhanded. She finally got the job, and I was disappointed, of course, but I really feel that I've helped to change the way things get done at the firm, and I've changed myself. Facing my own ambition made me much less frightened of my colleague's competitiveness."

## CHOOSING DIFFERENCE

Choosing competition means choosing difference. When men talk about competition, they talk about difference, about "knowing the difference between who I am and who you are." But for women, difference is very difficult. For women, difference can feel like loss of self rather than self-development. Separation can feel like betrayal, not self-assertion.

When women compete with each other, we are trying to differentiate ourselves. But since knowing we are different from other women frightens us and makes us feel that we will be abandoned and alone, most of us have learned to disguise our competitiveness. Instead, we feel envy. We feel envious of the women with whom we compete, far more consistently than men envy the other men they come up against.

Envy can be understood as a form of thwarted identification.* Envy indicates our desire for sameness, *not* for difference. Unlike jealousy, which indicates we are perceiving a loss, envy implies desire—the desire for a connection we feel is disrupted by difference. We experience envy when we meet someone who is different from us and, we think, better than we are. We covet what that person possesses because her possessions, whether material, physical, or intellectual, disconnect her from us.

Some women attract other women's envy the way honey attracts bears. They have only to walk into a room to make all the other women there miserable—hating themselves, loathing her.

Elena, twenty-five, is such a woman. She is exceptionally beautiful. Her long, luxuriant blond hair, her large eyes and sensuous mouth, and her lean body provoke instant antagonism from other women. "No matter what I do," she says, "no matter how nice I try to be, other women hate me."

Elena's statement, while heartfelt, provokes little sympathy from most women. We hate her because we can't identify with her, because she has too much, because she is what men want and we're not. We envy her because we can't connect with her—she is *too* different.

---

* The idea of envy as a form of thwarted identification is particularly relevant to the work of psychotherapists in the Kleinian school of object relations.

*Envy*

Yet it is far easier for most of us to admit that we envy another woman than to recognize that we are competing with her. Even a thwarted identification is still an identification, but recognizing competition is admitting difference, separation—and defeat.

Men don't have this problem. When men compete with each other, they compete to identify with a masculine ideal embedded in their competition, to be strong, tough, aggressive, independent—and separate. Unlike a woman, a man can make his competition impersonal because he can detach it from the man who is his current antagonist. Although we may not admire some of the ideals offered to men, all these ideals encourage men to become self-determined individuals.

The issue at the crux of our competition is that, traditionally, we suffer from an absence of self-defining ideals for female life. We are taught to be generous, kind, nurturing, compassionate, sensitive, egalitarian, and empathic. But what we've been taught has weakened, not strengthened, us. We are encouraged to give up self-determination, and instead to develop an ethic of self-sacrifice.

*women's Ideals*

There can be no question that all of the qualities women are taught are virtues, or that men as well as women should develop them. But when women embrace these ideals, all too often we use them as coping mechanisms to allow us to fit into a society that disparages us. Rather than enhancing human connection, we are taught to practice our ideals as forms of submission.

Compassion and fairness are two good examples. Although we can be extraordinarily compassionate, usually we are compassionate only to certain people in certain situations—men in general, children in general, other women in trouble. As Elena and other beautiful women discover, we have real difficulty extending our compassion to success.

Further, when women try to be "fair," we usually do something that sacrifices ourselves. For example, David, forty-four, a Washington, D.C., attorney who spends much of his time attending highly charged political meetings, notes that it is the women at the conference table who wait to hear other people speak, while the men generally insist on speaking first, longest, and loudest.

Yet David adds, "There have been so many times when I'm dying to hear what a woman has to say because I know that her talents and intelligence could be crucial to solving a particular problem. But she hangs back, waiting for a legitimate break in the conversation. I've seen women lose their chance to speak at all in the effort to give everyone a fair hearing."

Most women do not practice ideals actively, nor are we supposed to. We practice our ideals *reactively*. All of the virtues that should be women's ideals can be subsumed under one label: endurance.

Reactive ideals are like old-fashioned piecework. One patches a whole life together out of the fragments left by other people. And, as with piecework, there is a lot to do but the pay is low and the exploitation high. However, without ideals to provide a vision of an alternative life, most of us have no idea what we want to be *after* we differentiate. Many of us even realize that winning a competition means becoming more like a man—not more like a woman.

One of the main efforts, as well as a major triumph, of the feminist movement has been to tear through the veils of social assumptions about women. The feminist movement is inductive, not deductive. Feminist theories grow out of real life experiences reported by individual women, who, with support, finally are able to speak about what they couldn't even think before.

The feminist movement is making our society more humane in a very particular way. Like the civil rights movement, it encourages consciousness and supports multiple realities. It offers us hope.

But consciousness means recognizing that all women are not the same. We tend to assume, in the deeply intimate conversations we have with each other, that every woman's story represents all women. Yet the price we pay for such bonding is unconsciousness. We confuse intimacy with sameness and therefore deny multiple realities.

When we deny our own competitiveness with each other we feel bonded and intimate, but we also deny the reality of our individual lives. Some women want power; some don't. Some want children, or men; some don't.

When we assume that bonding with each other depends on denying individual desires, we impose our own versions of reality on each other, and by doing so, we lose choice.

For example, Molly, thirty-four, teaches in the women's studies department of a small private university. "For the longest time I couldn't understand why two of my senior female colleagues seemed so suspicious of me," she said. "Then I realized that it was because I like to wear dresses and some makeup, and they don't. I thought it was a question of likes and dislikes. I also thought that feminism meant choice. They thought I was betraying them. It didn't even have to do with flirting with the men in our department— the women simply wanted me to look exactly like them. As long as I wore what I wanted, I wasn't a sister."

When we realize that consciousness is based on tolerating difference, we can choose how we want to be different, and learn to distinguish difference from betrayal. We can choose how we want to compete.

## NEGATIVE COMPETITION

Writing this book, I learned that choosing competition means learning to regard it as a neutral activity, one that women as well as men perform. When we think about competition as neutral, we erase the boundaries between the categories that separate women from each other. Thinking of competition as neutral changes "bitches" into women who compete.

When we think about *how* we *should*, rather than *why* we *should not*, compete, we can figure out, quite consciously, how to make our competition part of the way we relate to each other. But in order to do so, we need a new definition of competition, one that allows competition to serve both self and other. We need new ideals that will allow us to remain connected *while* we compete.

Since the ideals we live with are about subordination and self-sacrifice, we have to make up our real life relationships with each other as we go along. We have to figure out how to maintain a balance of power mutual enough to *have* a relationship.

Mutual power is a fundamental necessity in good relationships, between friends, spouses, lovers, and colleagues. But women have a very shaky history with mutual power. Most of us have never experienced relationships based on mutual power, even with our friends.

Alanna, forty-three, and Martine, forty-six, met ten years ago, when both were attending a seminar for creative writers. Although each was writing a novel, they felt a natural affinity strong enough to override the inherent competition between them, and eventually became good friends, sharing the ups and downs of writers' lives.

But "our relationship fell apart just recently," Alanna told me. "I'm still not sure why. We both need money—all writers do—so we each teach creative writing occasionally. Those jobs are very competitive, since there are so few of them. I heard about a good one, and called Martine to tell her. I feel that's what friends do for each other—make a community, share the news, even if it means cutting into your own chances.

"So I was shocked," Alanna continued, "when I found out that Martine called the interviewer and got the job before I could even put in an application. Knowing she could do that has changed everything. How can I trust her now?"

As Alanna tells the story, she sounds like a hero. She practiced a set of values informed by cooperation, integrity, and general fair play. And her surprise at Martine's underhandedness confirmed that she would never act that way herself.

But Alanna is not quite so innocent as she believes. In reality, when she called Martine, she set up her own betrayal. She created a test of friendship for Martine, but it was a test she implicitly begged Martine to fail. While Martine was competing for a *job*, Alanna was competing for power—the power of being the "best" friend. Unable to acknowledge how much she herself wanted the job and how much she feared being rejected, Alanna unconsciously decided that if she couldn't have the job, at least she could confirm her own virtue. She used her friendship with Martine to give herself power—the sort of power that makes us despair about the world and feel terrible living in it.

Alanna certainly is right when she says friends need

cooperation and community. But if she had acted out genuine community with Martine, the two would have had a very different conversation. Instead of simply telling Martine about the job, Alanna should *also* have told her friend how much she herself wanted it, and how much she feared being rejected. *Then* Martine could have made a choice about competing with Alanna, as well as had a real chance to live up to the friendship both women shared.

Alanna practiced *negative* competition with Martine. It creates a constant imbalance of power in women's relationships. In the most typical version, each woman competes to tell the sadder story, to be the most victimized. Negative competition is the fundamental reality of relationships between women in a society where they have access only to indirect social power. When we practice it, we seek reassurance and consolation precisely from the other women with whom we are competing.

For example, last summer my sixteen-year-old daughter asked me why so many of her friends insisted that they were "fat," when clearly they were not. In part, they wanted her to console them about an anxiety all women in our society feel, sooner or later. However, they were also competing with her, since her natural slenderness made them even more anxious than usual. Although she did her best to reassure them, *she* was left feeling somehow failed, as if she'd lost a competition none of them could acknowledge.

In other women, negative competition takes different forms. Some women constantly "mother" other women. While they perceive themselves as kind and nurturing, the women they mother may regard them as overbearing and domineering.

Some women convince themselves that other women are more attractive, successful, and competent than they could

ever be. They make a virtue out of feeling inferior, while
making the other women uncomfortable about issues they
may not even care about.

Some thrive on martyrdom. At home they cook all the
meals for their families *and* clean up. At their offices, they
do *all* the work, both their own and much of their colleagues'. They feel overworked, overburdened, unappreci-
ated, and exhausted all of the time.

Female martyrdom is different from the masculine
"workaholic" version. Unlike men who work too much
and too hard, female martyrs usually don't receive the male
rewards of status and money. Instead, their compensation
is competitive victory over other women.

Leah, forty-eight, is the office "martyr" at a large advertising agency where everyone is under constant pressure to
produce.

"My office is directly across the hall from Leah's," said
Claire, one of her colleagues. "I see how hard she works.
She never stops, not even to knock off for a cup of coffee.
But I also see that she gets a lot of sympathy. Other women
in the office are forever dropping by, standing outside her
door, commiserating with her and trying to get her to take
better care of herself. Although she doesn't ask for sympathy directly, it's clear to all of us that she needs help.
She doesn't ask, but she makes the rest of us feel like we
barely work at all because she takes on so much more than
we do."

But if you asked her, the last thing Leah would say about
herself is that she is a competitive woman. Instead, she
believes that she is helping her female colleagues by doing
more than her share, lightening their load.

Yet, like Claire, the women in Leah's office know that
when she overworks herself, Leah competes with them. She

competes for the power inherent in working too hard and doing too much. She competes for sainthood.

In turn, they compete with her—and lose. When they sympathize with her and console her, they tacitly admit her competitive victory. They silently admit that she *is* better than they are. And beneath the sympathy they offer, they resent her.

Fundamentally, when women compete negatively against each other, the first woman to experience a competitive loss is the competitor herself. Negative competition reflects the low self-esteem and insecurity most of us see in our mirrors every day of our lives. Competing negatively, we use our real talents in ways that translate strengths into weaknesses and self-assertion into self-denial. We resign ourselves to a competition for indirect power in our relationships with other women because doing so is less frightening than admitting that we possess powerful desires.

When we compete negatively, we demonstrate that we don't trust each other because we don't like ourselves.

## AFFIRMATIVE COMPETITION

A family-systems therapist, Edwin H. Friedman, writes: "The essential question of human existence is . . . how you can maintain your integrity—the struggle to preserve your own being."

Integrity, Friedman says, has to do with our commitments, "with what we believe, with what we treasure most, with what we would give our lives for, with what we would sell our souls for."*

---

* Dr. Edwin H. Friedman included this comment about integrity in a manuscript version of his recently published book, *Friedman's Fables* (New York: Guilford Press, 1990). The entirety of his published book bears out his comment.

In other words, integrity is about competing for ourselves *and* for our commitments.

Imagine a basketball game. On the court are two teams, each composed of forty- and fifty-year-old women. Set aside your desire to laugh at this picture. Notice instead that the ball is not dropped by accident. Realize that these women could play much better *if they wanted to*. Listen to the level of noise. Hear the constant chatter and much embarrassed laughter. These women play because they're having fun *playing*, not winning.

Now imagine the same court, same game, but this time the players are all women between the ages of fifteen and twenty-five. Notice that you're not laughing now. The level of skill appears much higher. When these women drop the ball, *they don't want to*. Listen to the level of noise: it comes from the fans, not the players. These young women play because *they want to win*.

Now think about the two games. If you're a woman over forty, you celebrate the way the older women play the game. You know that they don't play well because they want to play together.

However, if you're a woman between fifteen and twenty-five, you have real trouble suppressing your irritation at the older women, running around the court like a bunch of "ditses."

But both sets of players are doing something right. When the older players insist, by their fumbles, that connection with each other is more important than winning the game, they teach their daughters about female community. When the younger players take the game very seriously and play to win, they teach their mothers that winning and community do not have to be separated. They teach their mothers about integrity.

In our imaginary picture of the younger women's game, we failed to see that when one young player made an error, all the other members of her team rushed to her, stroking her hair, patting her shoulder—offering instant comfort. We missed it because it happened so quickly. The players returned immediately to their places on the floor.

The young players act in a way that makes us remember part of the Latin root of the word *competition*—to strive *together*. They teach their mothers that striving to win and to excel is *part of their connection*. They've absorbed, unconsciously, as part of their personalities, the very conscious struggles performed by their mothers to achieve self-definition and self-determination. They are living evidence of the success of the feminist movement. They are both self-determined *and* connected to each other.

These young women are exploring territory their mothers, because of their place in history, were able only to imagine. They no longer accept the maps drawn by men that tell them that their competition with each other must be coldly impersonal in order to succeed. They are redrawing the boundaries dividing the personal from the impersonal and creating new frontiers for women by competing *openly and personally*.

These young women demonstrate, in their lives on and off the basketball court, how competition between women can act as the agent for change in the larger society. When they compete openly, they make their anger visible. They explode the category we put angry women into. They teach us that angry women are women who know what they want and know they don't have it. They know that women

Use of anger

can use anger just the way men do—as energy to meet a challenge.

They teach us that *we compete well only with people we trust.* They explode the patriarchal myth of women's fundamental lack of integrity.

Rachael, sixteen, spoke for both generations when she said, "I only compete with people I care about and respect. Otherwise, when I win, it doesn't seem to count."

But for women in their forties and fifties, Rachael's simple statement seems very confusing. Arriving at her idea has taken them down a long, hard road. In their lives, caring for another woman meant *not* competing with her. Respecting another woman meant feeling too insecure to compete with her.

Only after examining their relationships with their own mothers could these women realize that when they care, they compete—they compete with their mothers.

But Rachael's generation is more fortunate. *Their* mothers, now in their forties and fifties, produced daughters who understand that self-assertion is a good, not an evil. In their own struggle to define themselves, these mothers taught their daughters that self-determination depends on competition.

So Rachael's generation trusts that the other women they care about and respect want, just as they do, to assert themselves. They know that *when you care, you compete.* That way, each woman enhances her own development while challenging another woman's growth.

These young women act out a different reality: they know that competition means connection. Competition makes them visible to themselves and gives them the ability to act on and in the world. They help their mothers under-

stand that only when you exist for yourself do you have
sufficient self-esteem to support anyone else.

## COMPETING FOR SIGNIFICANCE

Today more and more women are realizing that genuine
self-esteem produces a different kind of competition, aimed
at affirmation, rather than destruction, of self and other.
They are changing social ideas defining women.

Women's status, traditionally, has been ascribed, not
achieved. Women were born into the position they would
hold for the rest of their lives. Change came about because
some external force—a fairy godmother, a prince—
brought it to us.

Ascribed status made us believe that our lives were deliv-
ered to us; we did not have to go out and seek them. In fact,
we were not allowed to do so. All the quest narratives focus
on young *men* leaving home to find their fortunes. Even
today it is difficult, although more possible, to find a film or
book about a woman who goes "on the road."

But because we were told we had to stay at home, we
came to believe that if we left, we would fail. Kathleen,
forty-seven, now head of the successful management consulting firm she started herself, stated it well: "All too often
I've pulled my punches. The prospect of trying my best and
not doing well was more than I could bear."

Kathleen echoes a feeling that many women have about
achievement. Like Kathleen, many of us believe deeply that
competing for achievement means failing. Instead, we sub-
stitute ascribed status—being someone's daughter, wife,
mother, or lover—for any achievement of our own.

Yet Kathleen is a very successful woman, and her success

results precisely from getting out there and trying, from acknowledging and implementing the very hard work and competitive striving necessary to make women excel.

Somewhere along the line Kathleen stopped waiting for something to happen to her. She started to compete in a new way. She discovered that competition in general, but particularly with another woman, made her feel desperate.

Although Kathleen possesses real talent—as do most women—in making relationships work, she realized that in competitive situations she automatically and unconsciously limited her repertoire of interpersonal responses. Fear and nausea closed her down.

However, Kathleen reports, "Now that I know when I'm competing, I can calm myself down. Instead of acting on them, I use the feelings of panic and desperation as signals to think *before* I act. I'm more able to discuss common needs and outcomes. I'm not sure I'm interested in the common good. But I'm very interested in an outcome that serves my needs, like the need for challenge, change, innovation, creativity, and continuing education."

Notice that when Kathleen talks about outcomes, she does not focus solely on the bottom line. Her goals in competitive situations are linked to self-development also. Like sixteen-year-old Rachael, she competes for integrity as well as for financial gain.

Professional women like Kathleen are forced to realize that competition with other women is a reality in their lives, but they are changing the rules governing workplace competitions by making them both open *and* personal.

Kathleen's focus on competing for self-development keeps her competitions personal. Because her desires extend beyond financial success, she knows that if she annihilates her competitor, she will not develop. Her goals mean that she is as interested in the process of competition as in the final consequence.

The sense of themselves women develop by participating in a competition focused on challenge and creativity, on innovation and continued growth, is producing strong people who are not satisfied knowing that their success is linked inextricably with another person's failure. They want to succeed when others succeed.

They want the sort of creativity provoked by stimulating the creativity of others. They are competing to create a community where everyone thrives.

Right now, our society functions according to an economic model of scarcity. We believe that there is not enough to go around, that big fish *must* eat little fish, that competition is a zero-sum game.

Our characters—our beliefs, values, principles, desires, fears, and the action based on them—are the intermediary between our economic system and our ideals. As Erich Fromm says in *Beyond the Chains of Illusion* (page 121), if our characters change, in turn the ideals we live by and the economic conditions that realize those ideals also change.

When women compete out in the open with each other, they become aware that a model of scarcity provides them with little or no satisfaction.

For example, Marjorie, thirty-six, recently won a tenure-track position in the English department of a large university. She discovered, however, that her victory caused her real ambivalence.

"Since graduate school, my training directed me to this position," she said. "I was taught, and I believed, that jobs were scarce as hen's teeth, and that I should do whatever I had to, even undermine another woman, to get one. So I got my job, but now I realize that getting it meant accepting that if I won, two of my female colleagues, each as competent as I am, had to be shut out of the department.

"Now I feel really awful. We're supposed to be humanists in my department. How can I teach my students to value human life and dignity when the academic institution insists that my two colleagues are nonpeople?

"Because I won the competition, I feel implicated in their policies," Marjorie continued. "I can't really say that I'm not glad to have this job, but at the same time I know now, since I sit in at meetings I was excluded from before, that the department could have figured out a way to keep all of us. They could have gone to bat to get more slots from the administration, they might have decided that all the positions should go to the best qualified people, instead of tacitly accepting that they could hire only one woman. They might even have created a really enlightened solution, like job sharing, or a combined administrative and teaching position. Instead they accepted that if one of us got hired, the others had to go.

"And the worst part is that we three accepted it. The hiring process took four months. Not once during that time did we ever get together as a group. Each of us was too afraid to make trouble, and be the one to lose the job. One of my former colleagues was a friend, yet I accepted that my job meant she would have to leave. I don't know what she's doing now. I'm too ashamed to call her."

When Marjorie acknowledges that her own competitiveness helped to perpetuate a system that excluded other women, she takes one step forward. Gradually, as women compete openly and personally with each other, they are developing a new female character—one based on combining self-assertion and human connection. The economic model of scarcity doesn't fit. Instead, the economic system can be reconceived as a model of plenty. This does not mean that poverty will vanish, or that many of us still won't have less while a few of us have more. It doesn't mean that everyone will get what she or he desires.

It can mean, though, that we'll be able to believe that what's good for others is also for our own good. It can mean that, like Marjorie, we begin to understand that when our victory destroys another woman, we lose too. It can mean that we learn to believe that cutthroat competition is an aberration, not a law of nature. Living conditions change when our ideas about them change.

Women have been trained to feel satisfaction when we act in ways that include, rather than exclude, other people. Now that women have at least some real power in our society, we can insist on keeping our competition personal—and taking personal responsibility for its outcome.

This is a very dangerous position for women. Since we are in a period of transition, women know that the clock still might run backward as swiftly as it moves forward. Taking responsibility for change in the system can mean lost jobs, lost money, lost love, and lost chances.

But, as men have long since discovered, danger can give life meaning. Courage gives life significance. For women, acknowledging our competition with each other is living dangerously. Being responsible for it is courageous. Changing our society—changing ourselves—is significant.

As the British novelist Fay Weldon writes in *The Heart of the Country*, "Unlike virtue, courage is not its own reward. It has results."

# Chapter

## 2

# Competition Between Mothers and Daughters

### WHAT DAUGHTERS KNOW THAT MOTHERS DENY

Everyone knows that mothers and daughters compete with each other—everyone, that is, except mothers. In the competition between mothers and daughters, it's the daughters who see what's really going on.

One late afternoon last winter my daughter, then sixteen, arrived home in a snowstorm.

"How are you?" I asked, concerned about her frozen feet and frostbitten nose.

"Why do you always intrude on my life?" she replied, instantly sensing competition over who's in charge of her life—and it had better not be her mother.

"Ouch," I thought, stricken, hurt, rejected, and then

doubled over with laughter, remembering the same exchange, word for word, directed nearly thirty years ago to my mother by me, her teenaged daughter.

But I don't compete with my daughter. No, it was my mother who competed with me.

Susan is Jennifer's mother. Jennifer is Susan's daughter. They don't compete with each other; I know that, because Susan told me so.

At forty-eight, Susan is a tall, sturdy woman with brown hair curling softly around her face. The dominant impression she projects is competence—here is a woman you would trust with anyone and anything.

Susan clearly is devoted to eighteen-year-old Jennifer, sitting beside her. The two women resemble each other in a way that supports the old adage that daughters look like their fathers, while sons look like their mothers. Although Jennifer is as tall as her mother, she is slender and delicate, conveying an impression of fragility and natural elegance. Yet Jennifer's delicacy is belied by a deeper resemblance to her mother. Both are strong and determined women, who know what they want and know that getting it means hard work and competitive striving.

Yet neither Susan nor Jennifer seems particularly driven. Instead, both are pleased to be resourceful human beings—women with emotional and intellectual resources and the desire to use them well. Their achievements are linked directly to their powerful desires and to their ability to make long-range plans to get what they want. After much hesitation, both recognized their competitiveness as a strength, not a weakness.

But not their competition with each other. When I asked

about competition between them, Susan cringed. "The idea of any hostility between Jennifer and me is so threatening that if it's true that I'm in competition with her, it's so suppressed I don't feel it," she said.

Susan's comment echoed the feelings of most of the mothers with whom I talked. Thinking about competition with their daughters produced real mental and physical revulsion. The notion seemed to strike at the heart of what being a good mother was all about. Good mothers don't compete with their daughters.

But responding to the same question as a daughter, Jennifer told a different story, highlighting the conflict mothers and daughters experience in our society: "When my SAT scores came in, and they were pretty good, my grandmother brought over *Mom's* scores. They were better than mine. But the funny thing was, my grandmother didn't bring them to make me feel bad. She really wanted Mom to see that *her* daughter—Mom—was more successful than Mom's daughter—me."

Susan laughed, even as she winced at the memory. "I forgot about that," she admitted. "It was almost surreal, two mothers competing against each other about their daughters' achievements, when I was one of the daughters *and* one of the mothers. And if you asked my mother about competing with me, she wouldn't know what you were talking about. My mother has always thought of herself as completely self-sacrificing. She thinks of my sister and me, and now our families, as her whole life."

When we become mothers of daughters, we erase what we experienced as daughters ourselves, the knowledge that daughters don't necessarily trust their mothers. As mothers, when we fail to recognize competition with our daughters, we protest the fundamental distrust we felt, and often feel well into adulthood, toward our own mothers.

The distrust daughters feel toward mothers is encoded in the script written for family life by a society that needs to separate women from each other, while appearing to support the mother-daughter bond. Competition with their mothers is what daughters learn first and know best. It is the tie that binds mothers and daughters together in a culture defining women primarily through their relations to men.

Even today, despite the increasing numbers of women whose achievements expand their identities far beyond romance, competing with another woman for a man remains fundamental to most women's lives.

The distrust between mothers and daughters surfaces in psychological literature describing the "suffocating" mother. It appears in the contradiction between the sentimental ideal of motherhood we adore in our society, and the real-life experiences of adult daughters whose visits to their mothers begin with apprehension, exist through anxiety, and conclude with relief.

As a society, we long for our mothers. Even when we become mothers ourselves, even when we become acutely aware of the gap between motherhood and mothering, we yearn to incorporate into our own lives the mothers we dreamed about when we were children.

We long for a traditional family life that existed, for most of us, only in our imaginations.

A traditional family, we imagine, means a father who heads the household because he is the major source of income, and a mother who functions within the house as the source of support, kindness, and nurturing. Our image tacitly accepts the balance of power on which this family is based, with father at the top and mother subordinate.

This picture is deeply flawed, both in terms of the real experience of family life and the misuse of power, as has been reiterated insistently by contemporary psychologists and sociologists, particularly those working on women's issues. Yet, as an ideal, the notion retains enormous power over our hearts and minds.

For example, as recently as 1989, in an article entitled "The 'Mommy Track' Isn't Anti-Woman," Felice Schwartz, founder and president of Catalyst, an organization devoted to women's development in the corporate workplace, described traditional mothers like this:

> Ironically, although the feminist movement was an expression of women's quest for freedom from their home-based lives, most women were remarkably free already. They had many responsibilities, but they were autonomous and could be entrepreneurial in how and when they carried them out. And once their children grew up and left home, they were essentially free to do what they wanted with their lives. Women's traditional role also included freedom from responsibility for the financial support of their families.

Clearly, Felice Schwartz never met my mother, or the millions of women like her. In contrast to the romantic picture Schwartz paints, their "many responsibilities" were mainly work that had to be done over and over again, work gaining them almost no recognition and little emotional support. After all, *they* were supposed to support us.

And while Schwartz may have been describing upper-middle-class and wealthy households, where the mother supervised instead of engaging in daily hands-on cleaning and cooking, we now see such supervision for what it was—exploitative, not "entrepreneurial." And we can see that when mothers decided to make the peanut-butter-and-jelly sandwiches *before* making the beds, their decisions had little to do with autonomy.

Perhaps Felice Schwartz is competing with her mother?

Like Schwartz, many professionally successful women now between forty and sixty feel conflicted about their success. It interferes with the dream of traditional family life.

For some, resolving the conflict means justifying, as Schwartz unconsciously does, their own success by revising the terms of their mothers' lives.

For others, it means failing just at the point when success seems inevitable. It means paralyzing bulimia, crippling PMS, disastrous migraines. In traditional family life daughters are not supposed to compete *well* with their mothers.

There are no models in our literature and mythology with whom rebellious daughters can identify. While in her guts a daughter knows that she's in competition with her mother, she is told covertly that surpassing her mother can be very dangerous. If she betrays her mother, she may be abandoned.

Unlike sons, who are encouraged, however indirectly, to challenge and compete with fathers in order to become adult men, daughters are discouraged from challenging their mothers; they are taught to deny their own experience and to keep the competition with their mothers secret. Daughters are permitted to compete as long as the contest concludes in an adult life reproducing the mother's life. They are allowed to compete until they become mothers of daughters with whom they will not compete.

Nancy Chodorow's work on female development helps us understand why daughters are able to recognize competition with their mothers, while mothers hotly deny that it exists.

Chodorow realized that since women are mothered by other women, it is very difficult for a daughter to form an identity of her own. In contrast to boys, for whom the distinction is relatively easy, girls grow up with selves defined as being like their mothers'.

But competition means difference. Because women receive the message that they are extensions of their mothers, difference—and open, impersonal competition—is very hard for them.

At the same time, daughters are fighting for their lives. Daughters fear that becoming adult women means living their mothers' lives. It is a commonplace to hear women entering therapy say that what they fear most is becoming like their mothers, while men generally seek help to become more like their fathers. Daughters are fighting for the self-esteem they feel their mothers gave up in order to become wives subordinate to their husbands, and mothers subordinate to their children.

For mothers, the situation is less heroic and more confused. They are caught in a fundamental paradox. At the same time that they want to promote their daughters' development, they must teach their daughters how to be feminine. They must teach their daughters that feminine women compete with other women, since women are defined by their ability to appeal to men. Feminine women don't trust each other because they assume that being feminine hinges on competing with another woman for a man. Yet somehow, a daughter is supposed to trust the "other woman" who is her mother.

We are more used to thinking about traditional family life in terms of its effect on sons rather than on daughters. Calling it the Oedipal complex, Sigmund Freud described how, in order to become a man, around the age of five or six a little boy needed to give up his attachment to his mother and instead identify with his father.

Freud did not question why we accept the sort of family that demands that boys separate from the parent who loved and nurtured them throughout their early lives. Instead, he accepted as universal the need for boys to enter the public world represented by their fathers, leaving their mothers behind, confined to a domestic space.

Freud also did not question the identification girls were expected to make with their mothers. He accepted that female development depended on a girl's identification with her mother *in relation to her father*. In effect, he validated the hidden trap that traditional family life contained for little girls. Identifying with their mothers meant falling in love with their fathers and made the competition between women for men seem like a law of nature.

Traditional family life puts mothers in a very awkward position. While they must teach their daughters to identify with them in relation to a dominant man, they also must produce daughters who are self-determined enough to leave their original families in order to create families of their own. Family life offers mothers two psychological mechanisms to solve this dilemma.

The first is hostility. In order to separate from their families, *all* children, girls and boys, must feel enough anger at their parents to desire separation. As we all know, it's impossible to leave something or someone for whom you feel unqualified love.

But in most families, the "mother position" is the lightning rod for daughters' anger. The anger daughters feel toward mothers is their necessary response to their need to separate, but it's not an anger equally parceled out between mother and father. Traditional family life assumes that mothers will make primary relationships with their daughters, while fathers are secondary. In fact, often fathers are used by daughters to disrupt what feels like an overwhelming and suffocating relationship with mothers.

Daughters aim their anger at mothers *by design*. If they were equally angry at their fathers, they would have enormous difficulty both perceiving "love" as the means to leave their mothers and finding a man to replace the father who originally stood between them and their mother.

But if daughters were allowed to become *too* angry at their mothers, they might decide that instead of escape, they desired a real alternative to their mothers' lives. They might decide not to marry at all.

So "mothers" are given a second weapon: their position is designed to evoke pity from daughters. As Sandra, forty-six, said, "The most awful thing my mother can say is that she sacrificed her life for me. And she says it whenever we argue. It makes me feel like I just want to crawl into bed and pull the covers over my head."

Pity is different from sympathy or compassion. Many daughters feel real sympathy and compassion for their mothers when they consider the way their mothers lived, genuine distress when they acknowledge the often oppressive conditions their mothers endured. But when daughters feel pity, they feel an emotion that entraps them: pity fundamentally denies equality. We pity those people we feel are weaker than ourselves, those whom we must help because they cannot help themselves.

When daughters become too angry, mothers evoke pity.

As Sandra pointed out, her mother uses pity *when they argue*. Pity makes daughters want to help their weaker mothers, help them validate their lives by making the same choices their mothers made.*

But it's one thing to talk about the emotions associated with family positions, quite another to think about the people who actually inhabit those roles. Most mothers are as uncomfortable and unhappy as are their daughters with the relationship they are forced to create. In order to live with the conflicts designed by traditional family life, mothers deny and erase the competition between themselves and their daughters, competition expressed through anger and pity.

Instead, they convince themselves that their daughters are "going through" a difficult stage; they stifle the desire to confront; they learn to manipulate rather than demand. They learn to wait for the time when their daughters will be mothers of daughters. They know that then, their daughters will understand.

## MY BODY/MYSELF: COMPETITION BETWEEN MOTHERS AND DAUGHTERS FOR SELF-CONTROL AND POWER

"It just makes me feel sick to compete with other women," said Mandy, eighteen.

Like most women, Mandy links competitive behavior with a variety of unpleasant physical sensations. Competition makes her nauseated. Her head aches. Her stomach hurts.

* A brilliant portrait of the hostility and pity used by traditional mothers to control their daughters is seen in the relationship between Martha Quest and her mother in *The Four-Gated City* by Doris Lessing.

Mandy is not alone; competing with her daughter makes Mandy's mother feel sick, too. The aches and pains women experience in competitive situations with each other are not accidental. In our society, mothers and daughters keep the secret of their competition by displacing it onto their bodies.

We all know that the ideal body type for contemporary women is long and lean, an ideal with which women are bombarded everywhere.

But we usually forget that it was not until the 1920s that thin women were considered attractive. Before that, womanly curves—large breasts and hips—marked beautiful women. Then, women with large bodies were not figures of fun. Confined more securely to domestic spaces, large female bodies did not raise the specter of female power.

As middle-class women began to leave their houses to enter the world of work, largeness became unattractive. Largeness looked too powerful. Increasingly, as the century wore on, women were directed to decrease the size of their bodies. Fat became a feminist issue. Yet even women who consider themselves feminists still admit that they are exceptionally prone to depression on days when they feel "fat."

Ellen, thirty-nine, is an unusually attractive woman, with shoulder-length blond hair, regular features, and a slim figure. Her career as a lobbyist for a large prochoice organization gives her tremendous emotional satisfaction.

Yet Ellen realizes, "I'm obsessed about fitness. But I have to admit that I don't really care about the strength of my body. It's really that I know that if I don't manage to jog every day, I look lumpy and feel swollen. Sometimes I can't get out to run until quite late at night, after work. Then it feels like I'm punishing myself, but if I don't do it I know that I'll hate getting dressed the next day."

Ellen is responding to an emotional connection between what she looks like and who she is. Despite her successful career, despite the fact that she lives quite happily with a man she loves, when she feels "fat," she feels out of control.

Unconsciously, Ellen is struggling to define the boundary between her mother and herself. Like most daughters, Ellen remembers that when she grew up, she and her mother were locked in a fiercely competitive relationship.

Now, even though she has not lived with her mother for many years, their competition continues, symbolized by the size of her own body. When Ellen feels "fat," she feels as if she is losing control of herself to her mother.

In part, Ellen's need to be physically attractive reflects the living conditions traditional mothers endured in our society. Since their financial security was derived from their husbands, and the skills they learned in their careers as wives and mothers were devalued by the wider culture, traditional mothers had real reason to believe that physical attractiveness could mean the difference between hardship and comfort, that their existence depended on what they looked like.

But in another way, Ellen also responds to a psychological complication resulting from the competition between mothers and daughters created by traditional family life.

For most women, the current ideal slenderness is possible only during a brief period in their lives, when they are in early adolescence, just before their bodies begin to grow into womanly shapes. Visit any high school in America, and you will wonder why the girls all look so good. They don't, but they do all fit into their clothes because, in general, women's clothing is designed with their bodies in mind.

Even for women in their very early twenties, already too adult for near-childish slenderness, the sense of failure and envy of thinner friends can be overwhelming.

Metaphorically, when women strive for slenderness, we seek to remain adolescent in shape. And the shape we desire reflects the time in our lives when competition between mothers and daughters is most intense, the time when separation becomes both a real and a terrifying possibility.

As much as daughters want to differentiate themselves from their mothers, they also desire to remain connected. Unlike sons', their identities depend on both separation *and* connection. So daughters often locate their bid for independence in the size of their bodies. As long as we remain adolescent in size, the emotional struggle for separation is conducted in the context of metaphorical connection, just as it was when we were really teenagers, living at home.

More than most women, Joanne exemplifies this dilemma. Now in her late fifties, Joanne raised four sons at the same time that she created a part-time career volunteering in her city's art museums.

From the waist up, in her lace-edged high-necked white blouse, her elegantly tailored boxy jacket, and beautifully coiffed hairdo, Joanne looks like a self-assured, self-confident woman. Today, she says, even though she and her mother meet frequently in the neighborhood where they both live, she believes that her mother no longer exerts any influence over her life.

But from the waist down, Joanne tells another story. Wearing a dirndl skirt reaching to her knees, opaque black stockings and flat-heeled black shoes with straps across the instep, Joanne resembles a television split-screen.

Looking at her, one sees the competition with her mother powerfully made visible. Her clothing reveals her conflicting desires to remain her mother's daughter at the same time she wants to be a grown-up woman.

And like her mixed-message clothing, Joanne's apparent self-confidence is belied by her tiny body, the weight and size of that of a fourteen-year-old girl. As long as she looks like her mother's daughter, Joanne can continue to believe in her own complete independence.

In our society, *all* women suffer from eating disorders related to the covert competition between mothers and daughters.

Shana, now thirty-five, remembered, "All the time I was growing up my mother complained and worried about my body. It was almost as if she believed that my body was hers—not that she owned it, but that it was literally *her* body. She was eternally anxious about what I ate—she watched me eat. And the conflict was always the same—I was too fat."

When Shana entered therapy, in her late twenties, she learned startling information. "My therapist asked me to bring in photos from my childhood, especially teenage pictures from the time when tension was greatest between me and my mother. When she forced me to look at them, to really see them, I realized that I never had been fat. Maybe you would have told the girl in those pictures to lose three pounds or so, but there was nothing abnormal there."

Shana also realized that her mother's excessive concern about her body size was mirrored by an equally intense focus on her own body. "She was forever on a diet, always wanting to lose twenty pounds. But she never did, until I went off to college. In the first year I was away from home she lost it all and she's never gained it back. In fact, now, at the age of sixty-five, she's very thin and petite. She goes to aerobics classes three times a week. And in that same year, my first away from home, I gained all the weight she lost."

Like Joanne, Shana and her mother were making an implicit connection between body size and independence.

The more separate from her mother Shana became as she grew older, the more unconsciously important it became to her mother that Shana's body diminish in size. But, in a manner familiar to many women, when Shana finally left home altogether, she and her mother switched body positions. Shana became large while her mother became small.

Although women are taught to feel more attractive when they are thin, the emotional and physical message conveyed by reduced body size is powerlessness. And that is no accident. Good girls are girls without power.

Yet when Shana began to lose weight in earnest, in her early thirties, she was shocked by her mother's reaction. "I thought that finally she would approve of me, would really love me. And she did say, over and over again, how wonderful I looked. But there was something about the tone of her voice which scared me. I felt as if the competition between us was about to reveal itself. I felt that my being thin threatened her in some way I couldn't put my finger on, and that during all those years when she told me I was fat, secretly she was pleased. In fact, even while she told me how terrific I looked, she tore apart the diet plan I was using."

Shana's story makes visible the real competition between mothers and daughters. Daughters are competing for the right to exist as women. They are competing with their mothers for self-control and self-empowerment. But they must do it in a way disguised both to themselves and their mothers. They must do it in a way that hurts them more than it hurts their mothers, because connection is as important to them as separation.

When Ellen forces herself to jog no matter how late it is or how tired she feels, she believes she is in control of herself. When Joanne chooses to wear a skirt of the same style she wore when she was a teenager, and makes sure it remains the same size, she feels in control. When Shana "diets seriously," she is able to cope. Daughters of traditional mothers come to feel that self-control literally means controlling their bodies.

But at the same time, competing for *physical* self-control permits daughters to hide their need for emotional connection. What we eat and when we eat it, how much we exercise and when we do it, what we wear and for whom we dress, reflect both our fear of—and our desire for—connection. Ironically, reducing our bodies diminishes our fear of separation by making us more attractive to men, even as it increases our separation from our mothers.

Fat or thin, we are bound by the same dilemma. Thinner than our mothers, we win a competition for self-control. Fatter than our mothers, we lose self-control. In either case, separation within a larger context of genuine connection is unavailable.

In this competition, daughters can feel that they live with mothers whose power is overwhelming. Yet, when I asked Shana to describe the mother who felt so powerful to her, she replied, "She's very insecure. She can't cope with strangers. She has a hard time with recognition, and always feels that she's out of her league at parties. At the same time, she's very uncomfortable when I'm visible. This comes out especially in regard to my taking any risks at all, socially or professionally. Even when she was so angry at me for being fat, I think I sensed that she was also somehow glad, because to her it meant I couldn't go very far."

## SEXUAL COMPETITION BETWEEN MOTHERS AND DAUGHTERS

When my daughter was nine, and I was thirty-six, we spent a wonderful week together at a beach off Long Island. The coastal regions in that area are very beautiful—endless stretches of white sand, waving fronds of beach grass, gentle dunes in the background; massive sea in front granting proportion and serenity. But one of the most perfect days of that vacation contains an awful memory.

It was around four in the afternoon, when the light begins to slant in, turning sand and sea and self red-gold. Time to pack our blankets and towels and head for home. Watching my daughter walk toward me, I was nearly overwhelmed by a sense of closeness to her—which made the next feeling even more startling. Suddenly, without understanding why, I felt enormous resentment, even sullen dislike, of the little girl bathed in the beautiful light. Years later, when my daughter became truly adolescent, I remembered that reversal, so ugly then that I had instantly made it unconscious.

What I saw when my daughter walked down the beach toward me was another woman. Her fashionable bathing suit combined with a trick of the afternoon light to make visible curves her body was years away from really developing. Seeing her, I experienced the same vertigo you feel when the car you sit in has just stopped moving while the car immediately next to you is still in motion. You're not sure where the movement is, and for an instant, you're paralyzed.

Seeing my daughter suddenly look like a woman produced exactly that feeling of paralysis. She was in motion. I was stopped.

The competition between mothers and daughters is not only a response daughters make to the triangle formed by their relationship with mother and father. Mothers also feel the tension, particularly when their daughters reach adolescence. We often forget that in their original versions, Cinderella, Snow White, and Sleeping Beauty were *teenaged* heroines. When daughters reach puberty, mothers can feel like wicked stepmothers.

This feeling is reinforced by a society that devalues aging women: it makes us hate our aging bodies and the younger ones that seem to emphasize our deterioration. It is an emotion to which all of us are vulnerable as we age and as our daughters become women.

Even women who don't have daughters, even women who are not mothers at all, experience these feelings. In our society, every woman is a mother by virtue of the message spoken everywhere that women and children go together. Every woman learns it, as well, in girlhood from her own mother.

All women are vulnerable to feelings of sexual jealousy toward younger women. Women with daughters are forced to experience this jealousy more concretely, and most, as I did, experience tremendous guilt and shame when they force themselves to face the jealousy they feel toward their own daughters.

Clearly, this fear is not simply irrational or unfounded. Women *are* often replaced by younger women because there is an unspoken general acceptance and approval of men living with and marrying women much younger than themselves. Stories of husbands "running off" with "bimbos" are legion: they are the war stories women tell, about defeat, betrayal, and treachery.

But what is hardest for us to face is that the younger women for whom our husbands leave us are not "bimbos"; they are, in some sense, our daughters.

In our society, women in motion are usually young. The most invisible persona one can assume is that of an older woman. When young people, men and women, walk into a grocery store packed with middle-aged women, they experience an empty store. Rarely are older women pictured in advertisements, movies, and TV programs as fully developed human beings, complexly interesting and filled with desires.

The English mystery writer Agatha Christie understood this phenomenon very well when she created Miss Marple. Christie knew that an old woman made a great detective because she could go anywhere and see everything—no one would notice her. Even the current television series *Golden Girls*, which goes a long way toward making older women visible, still calls them "girls."

Older women are not "the other woman." They are barely women at all. Instead, the "other woman," the great villainess of melodrama, soap opera, and our own divorces, is really our daughter. But because the sexual competition between mothers and daughters is concealed so carefully in traditional families, the "other woman" necessarily becomes *really* other—not related at all.

One of the most intense forms this competition can take is in the relationship between mother-in-law and daughter-in-law. Simply by marrying sons, which women inevitably are forced to do, daughters-in-law become "the other woman."

Connie, forty-four, now divorced from her former mother-in-law's son, recalls her confusion when, at the age of twenty-two, she tried to become the daughter of her husband's mother.

"She seemed very concerned about me—in fact, when we moved to the city where my husband grew up and where his parents still lived, my mother-in-law made sure our apartment was scoured clean, and she took me all over the city to shop for furniture. I couldn't understand why I felt so wrong all the time—ungrateful, sullen, and simply mean—until I realized that what she really wanted was that my house should look exactly like hers. Then there was war. I guess I should have gotten the message sooner, when Tim's mother objected to the style of my wedding dress.

"But after Tim and I separated, my mother-in-law was tremendously civil, far more courteous than she had ever been while we were married. Then a really hilarious incident happened which made everything clear.

"I ran into her about four years after my divorce, just after I remarried. The day before, my new husband's picture had been in the newspaper—he had given a press conference about his research for the government. He's quite handsome, as is my first husband. My former mother-in-law made a real effort to congratulate me on my 'gorgeous, intelligent' new man—her son's replacement. And then she went on to reassure me that *I* was more intelligent than my new husband. I realized that now, because I was divorced from her son, she considered me part of the family. She was competing *for* me against my new husband, the interloper.

"I also realized that if I had known about being the

'other woman' early on, I wouldn't have taken it all so personally. But it was clear, once we stopped competing for a man—her son—that I was a desirable daughter. And what's even funnier is that I think I will always feel that she's my 'real' mother-in-law, because the bond we created by competing so hard all those years made us very intimate."

When daughters become daughters-in-law, they experience in heightened and visible ways the sexual competition existing between them and their own mothers. But visibility doesn't always make the competition easier to handle.

In our society, sexuality in mothers threatens the way family life is reproduced. In order to allow daughters to develop their own sexuality, mothers traditionally were directed to move offstage. Their play, the one starring them as would-be mothers, is done, the curtain down. But no human being gives up his or her sexuality quite so willingly. Instead, covert sexual competition transforms mothers and daughters into stepmothers and stepdaughters. And while "stepmothers" are ugly old crones, "stepdaughters" become "bad girls," sensual and sexy.

In our society, the patriarchal family is unable to contain more than one sexual woman at any one time. Traditional family life, which makes the father dominant, asks mothers and daughters to choose between two equally untenable alternatives. They can form a loving relationship that denies sexuality to either of them, or they can assert their sexuality and enter a battle that will conclude in real separation. Since neither alternative is acceptable to most mothers and daughters, sexual competition usually goes underground. Instead of "crones," mothers become overprotective and overnurturing, eternally fussing about bodies they do not inhabit.

Instead of becoming "bad girls," some daughters translate their blossoming sexuality into excessive concern about
their weight. Others confuse sensual development with an
intense focus on their clothing or grooming. They dress in
ways their mothers hate, sometimes going out of their way
to select the sort of revealing clothes that advertise the
newly developed sexuality that challenges their mothers.
That way, both mothers and daughters are able to think
about their bodies, although, unconsciously, they are very
careful not to think about them with pleasure.

When daughters become daughters-in-law, the sexual
competition with their husbands' mothers is all too explicit.
Like Connie, many daughters-in-law find themselves
locked into a sexual battle with their mothers-in-law lasting
for decades. The new family they are creating contains too
many mothers. Either the daughter-in-law or her mother-
in-law must accept the role of "other woman."

Sometimes the sexual competition between a mother and
daughter can produce life-shattering consequences, extending far beyond the perimeters of nuclear family life.

Adele, forty-seven, is now a successful attorney within a
large corporation. But she remembers that an unwanted
pregnancy at the age of twenty-three, during her first year at
law school, nearly ruined her life. "I could hardly believe
it," she said. "I got drunk at my best friend's wedding—she
was my roommate at law school—and just went too far
with one of her cousins. I didn't even like the guy, and I
certainly didn't want to marry him. I didn't even want to
see him again."

But the bride, Adele's former roommate, believes that
the event was more complicated than Adele realized.
"Adele and I look very much alike—so much, in fact, that

several of my husband's relatives, who were meeting me for the first time, assumed she was the bride. I think this was very hard on Adele, because her own mother was not pleased that she had chosen law school instead of marriage.

"In particular, Mark's Aunt Millicent, a very formidable woman, was especially hostile. You could feel the negative tension across the room when she and Adele met each other. Aunt Millicent, like Adele's mother, is from the old school. She made sure to tell Adele all about her four children, her wonderful husband, and her lovely home. You could just see Adele turn white.

"I think Adele was much more interested in making a statement to Aunt Millicent than in the man she picked up at the wedding. Drinking too much was just an excuse. Adele really was showing Aunt Millicent that she could have a man anytime she wanted, even though he wasn't a man she liked."

Far away from her mother, Adele nevertheless responded to the sexual competition between them. Although she was able to terminate the pregnancy that might have canceled her law career, it took her years to absorb the emotional impact of her abortion, and it took even longer before she was able to cease using her sexuality as a weapon against her mother, years before she could link sexuality with pleasure rather than hostility.

Ursula Le Guin, who writes science-fantasy novels and feminist essays, talks in *Dancing at the Edge of the World* about the opportunity women miss when they fail to comprehend the power inherent in becoming a "crone." She urges women to revel in their "change of life"—to understand menopause as freedom from being any longer defined by their sexual attractiveness. She implies that sexual competition between women after menopause is revealed for what it always was—a struggle for power and authority. But revealing the real basis of sexual competition can be very dangerous for daughters. Cast by family patterns as the "other woman," they can be offered by their sexual development the sort of power and authority they really do not want. Daughters find themselves in a sticky situation. While their developing sexuality is the mark of their mothers' success *as* mothers, they often experience it as a danger to their mothers. They want to protect their mothers—from themselves.

Sometimes such protection takes the form of giving up sexuality altogether. Plump little girls become fat women, like Danielle, who at the age of twenty-five carries nearly two hundred pounds on her five-foot-three frame. Danielle believes that her mother gave up too soon. Even when she was a small child, Danielle was her father's favorite, far more special to him than his wife. Now, weighing too much protects all three of them from a relationship Danielle still finds very threatening.

For other women, the desire to protect their mothers from their own sexuality results in disastrous romantic relationships. Unlike Danielle and her mother, Tanya, twenty-two, and her forty-seven-year-old mother both are exceptionally beautiful women. But Tanya reports, with real distress, that her mother "is having a very hard time now. She was a model before she married [Tanya's] father, and since then she's been the kind of wife every man envies. That's been her job. But lately, she's been thinking about plastic surgery and buying an outrageous amount of new clothes."

Tanya admits that her mother's behavior makes her feel

guilty. She realizes that, somehow, her own beauty makes her mother feel very insecure. "I don't know quite what to do," she said. "On one hand, she really supports me, and I know she gets a kick out of how much I look like she used to. And she's still very lovely. But I feel as if I'm hurting her, and I miss the easy talking we used to do."

But instead of approaching her mother directly—"that would hurt her too much"—Tanya works out their sexual conflict in her own romantic life.

Tanya's pattern with men evokes a chord of recognition in many women. Between the ages of eighteen and twenty-two she has "fallen in love" four times, each time breaking up the relationship just when the romance was at its peak. Yet each breakup has devastated her. What Tanya experiences as love is really a problem of competition. Each new romantic relationship presents her with an unconscious dilemma. While having a new man means she competes successfully with her mother, satisfying her own sexual desires seems to betray her family's tacit direction that her mother should be "the fairest one of all."

So Tanya protects her mother by making sure that none of her romances endures. She wins one part of their competition, but loses another. Each time she protects her mother by ending a romance, Tanya suffers afresh from the devastating disappointment she experienced as the "other woman" in her family—the woman her father did not choose. At the same time, by making sure she is unsuccessful in love, Tanya validates her mother's success. Neither Tanya nor her mother is able to recognize Tanya's sexuality without feeling that it marks her mother's decline.

In effect, both Danielle and Tanya are distorting their sexuality in order to protect their mothers from a world set up by and for men. Unconsciously, they attempt to create a version of female sexuality circumventing the competition between them and their mothers. They attempt to mother their mothers.

This type of effort appeared in an even more unusual form when I talked to Roberta, thirty-six, a forthright and determined attorney, whose practice on behalf of low-income clients keeps her concentrated on large social issues such as poverty and homelessness.

Roberta's personal life reflects her unconventional professional direction. Roberta is a lesbian. She "came out" when she went off to college in the early 1970s, and since that time has lived with two women for periods of between three and four years each. Lately, however, Roberta has begun to reconsider her homosexuality. "Since I'm really not certain yet," she told me, "I haven't told my mother. I don't want to raise her hopes"—this last statement a wry acknowledgment of her mother's ambivalent feelings about her sexuality. "But I'm beginning to think that being lesbian was somehow a choice I made and it had more to do with my relationship with my mother than with my own desires."

Roberta is a member of a very tiny group of women who are privileged in an enormously ironic way. They became adults at a time when homosexual men and women could begin, at last, to acknowledge openly their way of life. This was a much needed, long overdue disruption of a tenaciously held prejudice in our society. But Roberta and the small sample of other women like her with whom I talked are discovering that this privilege was governed by the sexual competition they had experienced with their mothers.

Going to college in the early 1970s meant that Roberta participated not just in a new openness about homosexuality, but also in the larger context of militant feminism.

To some degree, Roberta's generation of college women lived the feminist revolution articulated and made conscious by women now in their forties and fifties. For Roberta, this meant that the conflicts about sexual identity she shared in late adolescence with most men and women somehow became confused with issues of political freedom and emancipation. Choosing homosexuality for Roberta meant *not choosing* traditional romance, meant abolishing, once and for all, the sexual competition for men that kept women separate from each other.

But what Roberta and women like her discovered as they grew older, as they faced their own desires for children and family, was that their choice had been made out of a strongly suppressed need not to compete with their mothers—particularly not to compete sexually. Not only would they forbid heterosexual romance a foothold in their lives; they would also retain their position as daughters. They would protect their mothers by not becoming mothers at all.

For many women who identify themselves as homosexual, this noncompetition with their mothers is not, of course, the dominant element in their sexual identities. But for some, for Roberta and the women who find themselves, like her, moving back to heterosexuality, the political has once again become personal. "What I feel now," Roberta said, "is that I have to figure out what I want—even when, let alone to whom, I'm sexually attracted—by figuring out how I can be my mother's daughter and also be a mother myself."

Like Roberta's, the hidden sexual competition most women experience with their mothers is reflected in the conflicted feelings they bring to other women. Winning or losing the sexual competition, women struggle with the same issue: how to be a woman whose sexuality does not inflict harm on another woman; how to be a woman whose sexual vitality does not disrupt her connection with other women; and how to be a woman whose sexuality does not betray her mother.

### PRESENTS MY MOTHER NEVER GAVE ME: COMPETING FOR BOUNDARY BETWEEN MOTHER AND DAUGHTER

"I was thinking about the gifts my mother gives me," said Joyce, fifty, during a conversation about mothers and daughters. "I just realized that she's still giving me the same things I wanted when I was a teenager. Even then, I think she gave me things *she* wanted. I know every time I asked for a bracelet or earrings, she gave me something either too young or too old for me."

The other women in this group, all in their forties and fifties, all with careers marking them as vastly different from their mothers, nodded ruefully.

"It's hard to complain about getting presents," continued Joyce, "but when I open a package from my mother I have this sinking feeling that I'm going to have to pretend to be grateful for something that really disappoints me."

Ruth's response was even more wry than Joyce's. "My mother gives me a white jumpsuit every year for my birthday. I can't decide if she thinks I wear them out during the year, or if she just likes white jumpsuits. In any case, I immediately give them to my daughter. There's no way I can put on a jumpsuit at my age, but they look great on a sixteen-year-old body. I guess my mother thinks of herself as sixteen, and me as her surrogate. She might even know that Carolyn's the one who wears them."

Even more than gifts of clothing, gifts for the kitchen

brought out their simmering resentment. "It makes me feel like she thinks I never cook—why else would she give me a standard skillet, as though I don't already have three," said Joyce. "My mother sends me recipes," added Lucy. "They go along with her comments about how skinny the kids look."

Listening to Joyce, Ruth, Lucy, and the other women in this group of well-educated, professionally successful— and, most of all, sensitive—women talk about their mothers, I realized that a tone of sullen resentment predominated. If I closed my eyes, I almost could believe that we were all fifteen again, gathered in someone's bedroom, getting more intimate to the degree each of us told a "mother horror story."

But the women I listen to are all grown-up. What's more, they are caught between a rock and a hard place. Each statement they make about their own mothers, they know with crystal clarity is made about them, by their daughters. At the same time these women are struggling to deal with resentment toward their own mothers, they admit that giving *their* daughters the objects they desire provokes feelings of discomfort, sometimes even disgust.

"I can't stand the clothes she wears," said Ruth. "I have to force myself to buy things I know she looks hideous in, even if they are fashionable. I guess I do want her to dress like me. But even so, when Carolyn wants to borrow one of my sweaters or blouses, I find myself resenting what feels like an intrusion."

Marlene's contribution made the terms of their two-sided conflict even more apparent.

"I sew very well, unlike my mother, who never did much domestically," Marlene said. "I decided that for her sixtieth birthday I would make her a wool suit I knew she would look fabulous in. She's sixty-five now, and I guess she's worn the suit twice in five years."

When I asked Marlene why this was so, she replied, with grudging realization, "The suit is in a style she never wears. It's really what I like. I suppose making it was part of my response to what happens when I ask her for something specific. Like last Christmas, I told her I wanted a new robe, in wool. She sent me one made of velour, short when I wanted long, and in purple. That's the way it always is. My coloring is redheaded, I look best in autumn colors. My mother is a pale blond, with blue eyes. She looks terrific in blues and greens, and of course, purple is her favorite."

Joyce, Ruth, Marlene, Lucy, and their friends are not really talking about gifts. They're talking about boundaries.

They fear merging with their mothers. Despite their status as fully grown adult women, they remain locked in competition with their mothers about their personal and domestic identities.

Despite their professional success, they believe that when their mothers look at them, the mothers see themselves. The daughters feel erased. They feel denied. They experience an enormous anger they feel forced to laugh about. What else can they do?

And they fear that they will pass on their anger to their own daughters, with whom, *as mothers*, they would like to merge.

What is the problem caused by separation and boundaries? According to Erich Fromm, it goes far beyond the focus on mothers and daughters. In *The Art of Loving* (page 8), he writes, "Man—of all ages and cultures—is confronted with the solution of one and the same question: the question of how to overcome separateness, how to achieve union, how to transcend one's individual life and find at-oneness."

Fromm implies that separation is, in some way, nonhuman. As a species, human beings find their satisfaction in groups, while "the awareness of human separation, without reunion by love—is the source of shame. It is at the same time the source of guilt and anxiety."

Fromm doesn't mean that men and women should not seek solitude, that they do not have real needs for privacy and aloneness; he does not mean that men and women are herd animals, but he does mean that being alone is related intricately to being together.

What both men and women want is *inter*dependence. We all want other people in our lives to whom we can commit ourselves and who we trust are committed to us. We don't want them to be physically present all the time, but we want them to be emotionally present forever. We want our children to call and we want our friends nearby. Fromm tells us that the events of our life and the choices we make answer, however unconsciously, the question of how separate we can stand to be.

Women learn very early that being alone is linked to being together. Women are nurtured by other women and taught to grow up to be like the women who are their mothers, so issues of separation and merger are primary in women's lives, as they are not for men. Women simply are not able to figure out how to live separately in the world by drawing a boundary defining them as "not-female," the way men define themselves.

Difference for men is easy in that their bodies differ from the body of the person who seemed intertwined with them when they were infants and small children. But women must define themselves simultaneously as female *and* as not-mother. Psychologically, this means that women develop fluid, permeable ego boundaries. The line we draw between ourselves and other people—especially other women—is murky and ill-defined.

In a way, as Jean Baker Miller, Carol Gilligan, and other feminist psychologists realize, such fluidity makes women stronger human beings than men. Because our identities depend on separation from *and* connection with other people, we develop the capacity to empathize to a far greater degree than men do.

But the murky ego boundaries women develop can also make the competition between mothers and daughters especially destructive.

Unclear boundaries frighten us; they make us fear that mother is daughter, and daughter is mother. Murky lines of demarcation produce overprotective mothers who suffer because they feel their daughters' pain as their own. They produce antagonistic daughters who suffer because they feel that their lives are suffocated.

In the traditional mother-daughter relationship, neither woman is permitted to develop completely; each must restrict her talents and abilities to fit her role. And each envies what looks like the other's freedom. Each is resentful at what feels like the other's power.

So mothers and daughters *use* the competition inherent between them in the patriarchal family to draw boundaries in the wrong places. They compete for the sort of separation neither really desires. They compete to define their roles, not themselves.

But at the same time we fear it, merger is the form of emotional connection encouraged for mothers and daughters. Unlike sons, daughters are not taught to become self-determined individuals. Instead of challenging their mothers, as sons are encouraged to challenge their fathers, daughters are directed to merge with their mothers, to satisfy their need for connection by paying the price of difference. But merger creates the indirect, manipulative, half-concealed competition mothers and daughters use as they try to figure out how to separate and remain connected with each other. It breeds the kind of competition that transforms generous impulses into emotional suffocation and gratitude into rigid resistance. Merger erases *choice*. It makes mothers and daughters feel that their relationship must be all or nothing at all; it makes mothers feel personally rejected by what really are statements of differentiation; and it makes daughters forfeit nurturing they yearn for in order to protect themselves from what feels like intrusion and invasion.

However, while mothers and daughters use their indirect competition to keep themselves from drowning in their merged attachments, they both fear that open and direct competition means too much separation. Open competition means exclusion.

When Joyce, Ruth, and their friends complain about receiving presents they don't want from their mothers, they really suffer from the sense that including their mothers in their lives means excluding themselves. Including their mothers makes them feel overwhelmed, while exclusion leaves them feeling selfish and mean. And deep within their hearts, they fear that excluding their mothers means, in turn, that their mothers will exclude them. They fear that if they draw the boundary around their own lives too clearly, their mothers will punish them with abandonment.

For example, Andrea, forty-three, remembers that she was nearly full grown before her mother stopped going through her handbag every night. "She thought she was helping me organize by clearing out all the debris. I wanted to tell her to stop, but I knew that she would be so hurt that finally I started carrying two bags—one that I brought home, and the other that I would leave in my locker at school," she says.

Traditionally, mothers and daughters are taught that open competition for identity is betrayal. The problem both mothers and daughters experience is that because they are supposed to share identities, neither woman really feels that the other is outside. Both mothers and daughters experience each other as somehow inside, part of themselves; thus, when they compete, there is no one outside to confirm the victory, to applaud and affirm their separate selves.

Although feminist psychologists are right when they suggest that the fluid boundaries women develop lend them a heightened capacity for empathy, ironically that fluidity precisely prohibits mothers and daughters from empathizing with each other.

Empathy depends on knowing that you are separate and distinct from the person with whom you empathize, so what could be, for mothers and daughters, a competition to understand and enhance each other's lives becomes instead a competition to dominate. Each woman feels—and fears—that in order to win, the other woman must disappear.

As Andrea put it, "Competing with my mother became much easier after she died."

## REDEFINING COMPETITION BETWEEN MOTHERS AND DAUGHTERS

Mother-daughter relationships reflect the wider inequality that women experience in our society. Just as mothers are usually subordinate to fathers, daughters are supposed to be subordinate to mothers.

When dominance and subordination are the defining elements in human relationships, the boundaries people draw between themselves and others are there to keep the dominant group in power.

Inevitably, members of the subordinate group are acutely aware of their status, while the dominant group usually confuses domination with protectiveness or concern.

"I really don't compete with my daughter," said Hannah, fifty-two, thinking about her thirteen-year-old daughter, Sarah. But Sarah disagrees. Sarah knows in her bones what she finds very difficult to say in words that won't hurt Hannah. Sarah knows that when Hannah tells her to wear a skirt when she would rather wear jeans, Hannah is competing with her about whose perspective on the world is "right."

For her part, Hannah is baffled. Why does a simple request to change her clothes cause Sarah to have a fit? "All I'm doing," Hannah says, "is making sure she doesn't look foolish. What's wrong with that?"

All mother and daughter relationships are not the same. Some mothers focus on their daughters' clothing, while others concentrate on their daughters' weight, or grades, or boyfriends. Sometimes variations occur within the same family, as mothers parcel out competitive arenas among two or three or four daughters. But all mothers and daughters sound the same theme. All daughters know, as mothers often do not, that the barrier between them is a competition for power and existence.

Daughters know that when their mothers tell them what

to wear, even if only to zip their jackets because the wind outside blows icy cold, their mothers are defining an experience not their own.

Daughters aren't always cold when their mothers shiver, they aren't always hungry because their mothers skipped lunch. Daughters sometimes even use safety pins as decoration rather than as instant repair work. Daughters know that these must be their own decisions. If the decision is their mother's, daughters know that they are not equal.

Mothers and daughters need equality in their relationship because unless equality is present, disagreement is impossible. Without equality, disagreement becomes invasion, suffocation, resistance, and unnecessary challenge: in short, a competition for power. Genuine equality means that mothers are recognized—and appreciated—for their real strength, wisdom, and experience, which are different from their daughters' and can be helpful *because* these are different.

At the same time, daughters are recognized—and appreciated—for qualities their mothers do not possess, and for experiences occurring in a world at least twenty years changed since their mothers were daughters living at home. When mothers and daughters realize that their competition echoes the traditional subordination of women in patriarchal family life, they are able to take much less seriously the family roles they have inherited. They begin to understand that their family roles define their *jobs*, not themselves. They begin to understand their competition as a tool they have been using to keep them separate yet connected—that they can compete for, as well as against, each other.

For example, Deanne, thirty-eight, realized that she and

her mother engaged in a lifelong competition to reverse their roles—but that reversal weakened both of them.

"I feel I have to look out for her; I always have," Deanne said. "But I'm beginning to think now that one of the reasons she's forever ailing, having headaches and other minor illnesses, is because that's when we relate best—when I take care of her.

"Lately, though, our relationship has improved dramatically. After my father died last year, my mother seemed to become a new person. In a way, it was very sad. They were married for almost fifty years, but after he died, my mother said she felt like a bird let out of a cage. She hasn't been ill since then. But we've had some wonderful talks recently, because now I feel that I can tell her about my problems. I don't always have to be the strong one."

After Deanne's father died, her mother flourished in a way unforeseen by either mother or daughter. The family roles they inhabited became less rigid as they redrew the boundaries between them. Their competition for power—in their case for who would give and who would receive nurturing—became less intense.

As Deanne discovered, sometimes a family crisis is necessary to force mothers and daughters to redefine their boundaries and their competition.

Right now, our entire society is having a "family crisis." Although statistics indicate that the divorce rate will decrease in the 1990s, most people today live in families radically different from the traditional model. As the construction of family life changes, so will the nature of the mother-daughter relationship. For example, some mothers and daughters live in households that don't contain fathers, shifting the balance of power between the women. Even when fathers are present, most mothers find that the larger social equality now available to women has tremendous impact on relationships with their daughters.

More and more mothers and daughters are rethinking their lives together. More and more mothers, now in their forties and fifties, are certain they do not want their daughters to feel about them the way they feel about their own mothers; they want to figure out how to live with their daughters in a way that brings them closer instead of pushing them farther apart.

The changing nature of family life means that mothers and daughters can choose to be together as fully developed individuals, that mothers and daughters can begin to trust each other.

It means mothers and daughters can figure out how to include each other in their lives at the same time that they do not exclude themselves.

Images of inclusion and exclusion, to symbolize periods of transition in women's lives, crop up frequently in literature written by women. What is inside also can be outside, like a window that one looks into and out of, or a door that is both exit and entrance. Alice Munro, a contemporary Canadian writer, uses such images in "Labor Day Dinner," a particularly vivid story about Roberta, a woman who has had the courage to leave a marriage whose terms excluded her "real" self.

Yet, when the story opens, Roberta is trapped once again in a romantic relationship with a lover who apparently wants to keep her "inside"—inside his house and inside an ego he attempts to make especially vulnerable to "outside" criticism. But Roberta has two daughters, Angela and Eva, who send their mother another message when they dress up for dinner in costumes they create from discarded window curtains packed away in the attic.

Ever since Charlotte Brontë wrote *Jane Eyre*, women have been threatened by the image of the madwoman locked away in the attic of the manor house, locked there because she refused to accept the terms of traditional female life. Now, Munro implies, the madwoman, confined inside, is out. Metaphorically unpacking the madwoman's trunk, seventeen-year-old Angela constructs a goddess costume, while twelve-year-old Eva drapes herself like a bride.

But each girl parodies the clothes suited to traditional female roles. The goddess is an adolescent beauty who ironically disdains the pedestal her costume places her on, while the little bride wears her shorts underneath so that she can turn somersaults despite her dress.

Both girls are inside their clothing but outside their roles. Using their costumes, they see "out" the window of traditional female life. They play with their roles, and teach their mother that "what isn't bearable can be interesting." They demonstrate that what's included inside need not exclude what's outside. To them, satire—or play—is the point.

Munro uses Angela and Eva to demonstrate that the permeable boundaries women develop in traditional families can be a strength as well as a weakness. Instead of understanding ego fluidity as merging, Munro sees that it permits mothers and daughters to draw their boundaries flexibly.

She is trying to tell her readers that Roberta's failed romance has as much to do with her own rigid conception of women's roles as it does with her patronizing lover. Choosing him, Roberta thinks she is paying dues she owes for leaving her husband, for transgressing the boundaries of traditional female life. However, through their costumes, Angela and Eva tell Roberta that, for them, she is a model of change. Her example allows them to turn somersaults in a bridal dress. Their example, in turn, teaches her that one can choose to be a bride *while* turning somersaults.

The relationship they create with their mother is inside and outside, give and take. All three women learn to see a door as both an exit *and* an entrance.

Angela and Eva are competing for their mother, not against her.

## "PLAYING" WITH COMPETITION BETWEEN MOTHER AND DAUGHTER

Munro's story has special relevance for contemporary adolescent girls and their mothers, now women in their forties and fifties. Because the older women struggled to achieve change in their own lives, many of their daughters possess a self-confidence unavailable to earlier generations of women. Like the daughters in Munro's story, often they are able to "play" with the boundary between mother and daughter, and since the world really is different, girls who now are between fourteen and eighteen have a forum in which to test their redefined boundaries.

Patrick Welch teaches in a large public high school in Virginia. He reports in an article in the *Washington Post* that many of his female students display "a greater sense of team play and cooperation than previous generations. The big difference that I see as a teacher," he says, "comes from the fact that far more young women now take sports seriously."

Team sports offer contemporary adolescent women the opportunity to compete and to connect with each other. It is an opportunity traditionally understood as crucial for young male development.

Athletic competition can be, simultaneously, inside and outside. Directed against an external antagonist, it generates group solidarity and cooperation. Directed within the group, it is translated into doing one's best, competing against the self. Still, team sports also offer young women a female community as well as a "team"—and a community of women is different in kind from a community of men. On a female team, individual players receive the sort of support that nurtures as well as challenges. Where male teammates interact through taunts or insults, women relate by applauding each other's strengths.

Melanie, eighteen, and Olinda, seventeen, are both members of their school's track team. Since track is the kind of sport where individual achievement is as important as team success, the competition among the girls can be as fierce as between rival schools.

Yet Melanie and Olinda agree that when they run in a pack during practice they try to get next to each other. "When Melanie is near me," said Olinda, "I know I do better. We're trained not to look around, but when I know Melanie's long legs are gaining on me, I run faster. I know that if I beat her time she won't resent me. And I get a real kick—it makes me want to do better—when she beats me."

Melanie nods, adding, "It's not just that running with Olinda makes me increase my speed. It's also that I know that the faster I run, the faster she'll run. I feel like doing my best helps us both."

Both women realized, with pleasure, that they looked after each other. "When I lose sight of Melanie in the pack,

I get worried," said Olinda. "I'm afraid she fell down or something."

"It makes me feel better knowing that we look out for each other," Melanie adds. "In a funny way, knowing that lets me compete better."

Melanie and Olinda are describing a female community, where the larger context of care permits each woman to shine. They have figured out how to make their competition affirmative, both by admitting it exists and by continuing to nurture as well as to compete. In fact, as their comments reveal, their competition itself has become a form of nurturing.

Playing sports, these young women demonstrate that competition and nurturing can be combined. Emotionally, they can be both mother and daughter to each other.

But since sport is big business in America, remembering that sport is play sometimes can be very difficult. Nevertheless, because women who engage in sports also engage in emotional connection, knowing that they are playing is not so hard for them. They want to win *and* they don't want to lose each other. Sometimes that means playing against each other, but as often, it means playing for each other. They understand play as the ability to shift roles, to exchange places, to be winner and loser, caretaker and cared for.

Melanie and Olinda's track-running experience highlights ways to change the secret and indirect competition mothers and daughters learn to practice in traditional family life. When the competition between mothers and daughters is openly acknowledged, the presence of the sort of playfulness apparent in women's sports can make a real difference between a relationship that is endured, although destructive, and one that is fulfilling and joyful.

Mothers and daughters need to recognize themselves as

a "female team" and to revise the rules of their game. They need to understand that only when they conceal their competition does it become deadly to them both, only when they feel their competition means separation *without* connection does it provoke the sort of anger that ends the possibility of all communication.

Traditionally, most mothers and daughters have played a zero-sum game—winner take all, loser lose all. Most mothers and daughters suffer from the feeling that confirming each other's victory means annihilating the self.

For example, Mary, forty-eight, remembers that she felt most like a loser when her mother insisted she meet the members of her bridge club: "It was very important that I act like her daughter—whatever that meant. She always acted as if I would embarrass her by being myself. By the time I was eighteen, I wasn't even sure I had a self."

In contrast, Melanie and Olinda, like other young women athletes, demonstrate that their bond is a competition through which each is affirmed, instead of denied. They applaud and support each other as competitive women. They are confirmed as individuals because their competition offers each woman a creative challenge. Through it, they forge new self definitions. They have learned that competition can enhance—rather than destroy—female community.

## MOTHERS AND DAUGHTERS, COMPETING FOR HAPPINESS

Who women are and what they want is no longer a mysterious subject. Women want to be grown-up, just as men do. They want to be responsible for the choices that define their lives.

Research indicates that when women feel they make the

decisions that govern their lives, however limited those lives seem to be, they are on the whole happier and less depressed even than women whose lives seem to be less limited. In other words, marrying the prince and living in his castle is less satisfying than building a two-room cottage yourself.

However, in order to make choices, women need to know they can compete—and sometimes even win—and remain connected to each other. A transformed mother-daughter relationship is crucial for this knowledge. When playfulness is part of the mother-daughter relationship, both mothers and daughters continue to develop and grow for the whole of their adult lives.

Cynthia, forty-six, and her eighty-three-year-old mother offer a version of such a bond. Cynthia understands that her professional success, as well as her successful marriage and good relationship with her own teenage daughter and son, stem from her mother's model.

"Mother was always what I would call a complete woman. She and Daddy would disagree, but she always stood her ground; it never got bitter. She competed with him, and with me and my sisters, quite openly. She knew her talents, and she never disparaged herself. And although she made it quite clear that she was disappointed when I chose to study economics instead of pursue her interest in art history, she also made it clear that I *could* choose. Because she was so forthright, I was able to understand that in some ways we're alike and in some ways very different. Although she has certainly become physically weaker as she's aged, there hasn't been real change in our relationship. She always depended on me, and I always depended on her. We love each other."

However, Cynthia admitted that this relationship was

not as easy when she and her two sisters were children: "Then, I think, Mother felt responsible for our happiness. She believed the choices she made for herself also would make us happy. But over the years, as we've all grown up, I've noticed that she no longer feels the same sense of responsibility. It's not that she neglects us, not at all, but she realizes that we are responsible for our own lives and our own happiness. In turn, that lets us know that she is responsible for her life."

Cynthia is talking about phases of evolution in a mother-daughter relationship, made possible because of the unusual self-esteem—for a woman of her generation—Cynthia's mother possessed.

Talking to Cynthia and her mother, I was struck by her mother's ability, even eagerness, to display her "real" personality in front of her daughter. She was as delightful and engaging with her daughter as I imagine she would be with her peers. She was a mother who also was a woman.

Because she was able to "play" with her role, so was her daughter. Cynthia and her mother competed to be the most charming, witty, intelligent woman around. Instead of competing to make each other happy, they competed to be happy. Because each applauded the other's success, their competition made them very good company indeed, both for themselves and for the other people in their lives.

Cynthia and her mother have learned that acknowledging their competition makes it feel like disagreement and makes possible a connection that feels like love.

As Erich Fromm writes in *The Art of Loving* (page 87), there is only one proof for the presence of love: "The depth of the relationship, and the aliveness and strength in each person concerned; this is the fruit by which love is recognized."

When mothers and daughters really love each other, they don't just endure each other. They compete for time to spend together so they can continue to use each other to grow up—forever.

For most mothers and daughters, of course, competing to be happy is a very tentative business. Like any new behavior, it takes relatively constant attention. It means being conscious of what we are doing even when we would much rather act out of emotional necessity.

For example, Emily, forty-three, believes that she and her fifteen-year-old daughter, Samantha, have a "really solid relationship." Emily says, "We joke a lot, and rarely have the sort of arguments that are about power. Most of the time, we're able to listen to each other because Samantha knows I respect her."

Yet, as Emily admits, it's all too easy to allow hurt feelings to interfere. "I'm divorced from Samantha's father," Emily says. "Even though he and I are relatively friendly, I've begun to realize how painful it is for Samantha when we're all together. I suppose it provokes her feeling of loss, even though we have joint custody and she lives with both of us.

"Samantha plays basketball on her school team. Both her father and I want to go to the games. I realized that Samantha was caught in a really tricky situation. She definitely did not want both of us there, but telling either one of us was a problem.

"Finally, I asked her about the excuses she was offering me about why I shouldn't come to the games. It was very hard to hear her say that she was choosing her dad instead of me. But at the same time, I forced myself to respect the boundary she needed to draw. She was serving her needs, and if I loved her, I wouldn't impose my needs on her, at least not in that situation. In turn, she appreciates my needs and makes a real effort to give me what I want, even when it interferes with something she wants.

"The point is, sometimes she can be my daughter, and I take care of her. Sometimes I let her mother me. Sometimes it's really hard not to say, 'Do this or that because I said so; I'm your mother.' But then I hear the sentence and I realize I sound just like my own mother. I don't want Samantha to grow up and think that calling me is a duty or obligation. The time to make things better is right now."

When Emily insists that respect is the fundamental quality of her relationship with Samantha, she means that they are equal. Each respects the other for her difference; each is careful about imposing her own needs. Emily and Samantha pay attention, not just to each other, but—even more important—to themselves.

When Emily forces herself to "respect" the boundaries Samantha draws between them, she also forces herself not to act out the anger perceiving those boundaries provokes. She pays attention to her own emotional state.

Emily knows that her anger, however appropriate or justifiable, covers up the far greater pain caused by Samantha's desire to separate. Respecting Samantha means facing her own pain, and constructing a relationship with her daughter that does not serve it. Paying attention, Emily is able to keep talking to Samantha. She and her daughter separate within a larger context of connection.

Emily and Samantha trust each other. They are learning that love, not power, keeps them together.

# Chapter

# 3

# *Women in Love*

Women are fascinated by love. But we don't talk about having it. When we talk about love, women talk about getting it and keeping it—or, in other words, about competition.

Katharine, forty-two, and Linda, forty-five, are having lunch together. Katharine teaches anthropology at a small private university; Linda is an attorney, specializing in corporate law. Both women are very attractive, interested in the world around them, in their professions, in books and music. They participate, to some degree, in the women's movement. They've learned not to define themselves solely through their romantic relationships.

Still, love is making them miserable.

"What bothers me most," said Katharine, "is the idea that I 'took' Cliff away from Janice. By the time I met him, they were separated. Cliff had been living in his own place for at least two or three months. In fact, *Janice* was the one who wanted the separation. Now she believes that the only reason they aren't still together is me. It's crazy."

Linda nods sympathetically. "I know what you mean. I suppose Peter's ex-wife, Marian, has more of a real grudge against me, since Peter and I met while he was still married. But both of them were terribly unhappy. After their divorce Marian lost nearly twenty pounds. She's dating; she looks infinitely better than she used to, but she just hates me. And she's still doing insane things—calling us at various times of the day or night, hanging up without speaking, telling Peter's two kids how awful I am. She even told their older daughter that I have AIDS—can you imagine! She just won't let go."

For Katharine and Linda, talking about love is the equivalent of talking about survival. It means trading information to place their love lives in the larger context of female life. "Do women really do this to each other?" and "How am I supposed to handle it?" they implicitly ask each other.

Talking about love means consoling each other, too. As they talk, Katharine and Linda reassure each other that they are not responsible for the hatred and fury each unwittingly seems to have unleashed.

Yet despite their desire to *feel* innocent, both Katharine and Linda experience a lingering guilt. There are children involved. Cliff brought his eight-year-old son to his new marriage, while Peter's two daughters, as teenagers, are at a particularly vulnerable stage. All of the children, as well as each of the adults, suffer from the torrent of emotional distress provoked by what seems to be women competing for a man.

Katharine and Linda really want to have a different kind of conversation, one much more difficult for them to begin. They want to discuss what they say baffles them. Although their confusion is genuine, it also is artificial. Signaled by their guilt is another knowledge, one they need to suppress. What Katharine and Linda know—and what they fear—is that if they were in the ex-wife position, they, too, might act out the anger coloring all of Janice and Marian's outrageous behavior. They might, even as they deplore Janice and Marian's doing so, hurt their own children to get back at the man and the woman who have hurt them, convincing themselves it is better that the children "know" how awful and treacherous their father is, how ugly and immoral their new stepmother.

Katharine and Linda aren't guilty about having a man— they are guilty about *not* having him. They are guilty about the fine line that separates women who are sane from women who are not, because they know, however much they silence their knowledge, that the rage expressed by Marian and Janice lurks somewhere within them as well.

Competition between women for men fascinates both women and men. Women fear that it reveals the key to their characters, because when they compete for a man they often feel as if they were acting against their own will, even against their desires, in ways that seem obsessed and downright crazed. And since competition between women for a man is part of the fundamental structure of traditional family life in our society, women are right: when they compete with each other for men, they act out a very old story, one women have not written.

However, even the men who have written the novels, myths, fairy tales, poems, and legends that say the best thing for a woman is a man yearn to hear more than women will ever consent to tell.

Men don't realize that the secret they believe women keep from them, really is kept best from women themselves. Most of us don't know we compete for men. What we know is that *other* women compete with *us*.

Most of us have absorbed very well the moral and ethical lesson directed at us in Western literature, particularly fairy tales such as "Cinderella," "Snow White," and "Sleeping Beauty." We know that a good woman is a woman who does not compete. She waits for a man to find her.

We know that competitive women lose—are losers—almost by virtue of their competitiveness. Competition makes women ugly, greedy, noisy, and unlovable. It makes them unfeminine.

Women who believe they are good women—and feminine women—also believe that they don't compete with other women for men. Even well-educated women like Katharine and Linda still practice Cinderella's version of noncompetition. They are baffled when other women accuse them of taking their man away. They believe that sisterhood precludes competition for men.

"I made a conscious decision that I would stop competing for men," said Kelly, twenty-two. "I finally realized that it was a matter of self-esteem, that the women who flirt with every guy they meet, no matter who he's attached to, don't like themselves. I used to do that, until I realized that I was shortchanging myself. Now I only respond to men if they show some interest first."

But what does it mean to wait for a man to "show interest"? As most of us know, but will rarely admit, it means showing him your interest first. It means nodding and smiling and paying him the sort of attention that you disguise both to him and to yourself as warm responsiveness.

Maeve, thirty-one, described her friend Celia as a woman "who walks into a party and gets every man's attention. She just radiates sexuality, but she honestly doesn't know what she's doing. She meets a lot of men, but she's always surprised when they want to sleep with her on the first date. She can't seem to put it together that they want what she seems to be promising."

Noncompetition doesn't work, and no woman practices it, not really. Like Celia, certain women seem to have an easier time than others attracting men. Lynn, twenty-five, is a good example. Her long blond hair, large brown eyes, and soft, overlarge mouth combine to make her an unusually pretty woman with a very sexy look. Other women don't like her.

"I get maligned immediately," Lynn said. "Everyone thinks I go with two guys at a time. Everyone thinks I'm a slut. I always feel much more comfortable if I'm not looking my best when I meet a new woman. It sort of dilutes the instant hostility."

Lynn's problem isn't new. Pretty women always have experienced it, but while most of us feel that women like Lynn have an unfair advantage, we don't realize that we give it to her.

Lynn's attractive physical appearance makes visible

what most of us don't want to admit about ourselves. Lynn makes us *feel* the competitiveness we bring to every encounter with other women. She makes us feel like Cinderella's stepsisters. Her existence exposes the lie of our noncompetitiveness. Simply because she is pretty, and, more significantly, sensuous, Lynn makes us apprehend what we would much rather deny: that in our society, a man stands between two women.

The noncompetition for a man appears in an especially malignant form in the behavior of some ex-wives, like Janice and Marian. Because they have convinced themselves that the "other woman" is doing the competing, they rationalize their behavior by understanding themselves as innocent victims. However, while their uncontrollable rage is directed at the "other woman," the woman they hurt most is themselves.

"I was just stunned when this happened," said Marilynn, forty-six. "I was dating a man who was separated, when one day his wife came to my office—which is private, thank goodness—and told me I should stop seeing her husband. At first she was simply angry, and then she tried to appeal to me on the basis of two divorced women, sisters in trouble, all that. But then, I think because I wasn't responding fast enough—I was really too surprised—she opened her blouse and showed me her breast. She said she thought she had breast cancer, but I know that she was showing me that hers were larger than mine."

Like the ex-wife in Marilynn's story, women who believe in noncompetition believe they are other women's victims, but Marilynn learned that sisterhood can be based on intimidation and fear. She learned that the woman to be feared is the woman who insists on her victimization.

## FEMININITY AND COMPETITION

Competition between women for a man is both a social and
an emotional process for most women: social, because finding and keeping a man has been, historically, the most
secure form of financial support for most women; emotional, because women have translated what has been an
economic necessity into a psychological desire.

Even though many women today don't need a man for
financial support, they experience their lives as somehow
vacant without a romantic relationship. Nevertheless, most
of those women lead lives filled with relationships, with
their children, their families, their friends, and their colleagues. But without a man, they feel desperately alone.

Having a man means competing with other women to
get him. Fay Weldon, whose satires of modern life are
brilliant and funny, describes in a story, "In the Great
War," how it used to be—and most women would admit
with pain, still is:

> Enid's mother Patty didn't stand a chance. That
> was in the Great War, in the fifties, when women
> were at war with women. Victory meant a soft bed
> and an easy life: defeat meant loneliness and the
> humiliation of the spinster. These days, of course,
> women have declared themselves allies, and united in
> a new war, against the common enemy, man. But
> then, in the Great War, things were very different.
> And Patty didn't stand a chance against Helene. She
> was, for one thing, badly equipped for battle. Her
> legs were thick and practical, her breasts floppy, and
> her features, though pleasant enough, lacked erotic

impact. Her blue eyes were watery and her hair frizzy and cut brusquely for easy washing and combing.

Weldon knows well, of course, that the "Great War," the war between women for men, continues. When feminist sisterhood became confused, in the 1970s, with man-hating, many women who yearned for autonomy and self-esteem understood that feminism was irrelevant to their lives.

In a peculiar way, they were right. The majority of women in this country still do not have a real choice about forming relationships with men. They are the women who go out to work every day in factories, in shops, and in other women's houses, women whose jobs do not pay them enough to feed, clothe, and shelter themselves and their children, and do not provide the emotional sustenance to replace even the hope of love.

But they also are the women whose jobs are professional careers, who have been educated at law school and medical school, who possess graduate degrees and financial security.

They know, just as Sigmund Freud wrote, that work and love are necessary for happiness, and they want both, just as much as they want female friends and self-respect. Even in 1990, they are the women who say, "I'm not a feminist," while they insist on equal pay for equal work.

The feminist notion of sisterhood missed a crucial point. Women are able to support each other only after they know what they want. And most women want men. But the feminist movement is right to argue that something about the way men and women relate to each other has separated women *from* each other. If women still fight the "Great

War," it is because victories still are won by "feminine" women.

It is because the relationships we imagine are about love in our society are really about power.

Karen Horney diagnosed the problem in an essay, "The Overvaluation of Love," which she wrote in 1931. She realized that feminine women think of themselves as very loving. In fact, Horney wrote, often "the feminine woman suffers from an entirely too exclusive concentration upon men. These women are as though possessed by a single thought, 'I must have a man'—obsessed with an idea over-valued to the point of absorbing every other thought, so that by comparison all the rest of life seems stale, flat, and unprofitable."

Horney astutely linked femininity in women with male desire. Feminine women want to be what men want them to be, but now women need to ask themselves *why* men want *what* they want. What is there about feminine women that is good for men?

Simply thinking about feminine beauty gives us the answer. Although conceptions of beauty change according to period and era—even the current ideal of feminine slenderness dates back only to the 1920s—the underlying reason directing the way women look remains the same.

Men want women to be "beautiful" in the ways that women's beauty is defined by men. And when one human being allows herself to be defined by another, she suffers from a loss of self-esteem because she experiences a loss of self-determination.

Still, although the feminist movement has taught women that being feminine hurts them, women know that most men still choose a "feminine" woman. As Karen Horney pointed out in "The Dread of Women," "The ever precarious self-respect of the 'average man' causes him over and over again to choose a feminine type that is infantile, non-maternal, and hysterical."

Therefore, getting a man, for most women, often is a question of negotiating for love, negotiating how much power and self-respect she will have to give up in return for how much love and how much security she will receive.

Femininity and competition between women are tightly interwoven. It is the feminine woman who really doesn't like other women. She can't afford to. To this woman, all women are rivals, since she has been defined by men in her person and her appearance. The woman who chooses to undergo liposuction, cutting and remolding her body according to externally imposed standards of beauty, does not just lose her thighs. She also loses her connection to all the other women whose thighs are thinner, and to all the other women whose fatter thighs remind her of her own loss—and pain.

Women compete with each other when they put on makeup, when they wear high heels, and short, narrow skirts that constrict their movement, when they dye their hair, and when they starve themselves. Femininity means looking better than other women—femininity means competition between women to look better to men.

The problem is that we all do it. We all pay attention to how we look and what we wear. We all want to look as attractive as we possibly can. Even good friends will assess each other automatically, rating themselves on an invisible scale that arbitrates a secret contest directing women's relationships with each other.

While femininity means competition between women, it

is also the dynamic connecting women. Giving up feminine behavior is very difficult because femininity means love. Femininity means loving one's mother. Just as a thousand years of Chinese daughters connected their mutilated bound feet with loving concern from their mothers, so women in America link the often painful details of feminine dress and style with receiving love from their mothers. For most women, being feminine remains a significant connection between mothers and daughters.

Yet, as Karen Horney discovered, the root reason why some women overvalue romantic love—and the feminine behaviors that secure it—is that it can be a way to separate from their mothers. Having a man, a daughter might feel, means she is no longer tied to a woman.

But overvaluing romantic love in this way is a defense, not a real change. Trying to get a man to stand between yourself and your mother makes visible the real dilemma femininity poses for women.

Karen Horney understood the conflicted situation created for women living within a patriarchy. Women, just like men, need to depend on and trust their mothers, but when mothers teach daughters how to be feminine, they teach them to distrust women.

The mixture of messages we receive is too much. On the one hand, we should depend on our mothers and grow up to be like them. On the other hand, we should be feminine, automatically distrusting *all* the other women who stand between us and men.

It's a dilemma that can make us feel confused and lost in an overpowering, hostile world. "I never know if I'm dressing for myself, for other women, or for a man," said Candace, forty-two. "Am I wearing too much makeup, too little, or should I forget it altogether? Basically, I just never feel right about what I look like. On bad days it can take me an hour to get dressed."

Some women attempt to resolve this dilemma by becoming superfeminine. Distrusting other women, they locate their hope for stability and connection in men. But ironically, the women who become extraordinarily feminine are trying to return to a woman. They re-create the distorted relationship they shared with their mothers by distorting their relationships with women *and* with men. Yet, as Karen Horney knew, the only real defense against a distorted dependence on one's mother is self-esteem. And self-esteem is precisely what superfeminine women lack.

## COMPETITION FOR MEN BEGINS AT HOME

We all, women and men, first learn about love at home, from our families. And what we learn can give us ideas about love—and about the competition to achieve it—that direct many of our adult relationships, sometimes for all of our lives.

Sigmund Freud believed that love relationships in the traditional family were based on the Oedipal complex, which he described as an emotional and erotic triangle among mother, father, and son. However, although he believed that he analyzed human psychosexual development, what he really described were the power relationships existing within the patriarchal nuclear family. What he analyzed were winners and losers in the game of love.

For example, when daughters win the competition for their fathers, they can be even more troubled than when they lose. Hilary, twenty-two, recalled, "My mother and my older sister were very close. I was my father's special girl. I always knew he loved me more than Mom."

But now Hilary is at least fifty pounds overweight, showing every woman she meets that she will never take away their man. As Sharon, twenty-five, acknowledged, "I won my father, but then I found out I didn't want him." Like Hilary, Sharon makes sure that the body language she uses—her baggy clothing, unwashed hair, and pasty skin—conveys that all her current rivalries with other women are doomed to fail.

Yet another consequence of "winning" Father is familiar to many women. It happens to women who find themselves falling in love with men who are "trouble," men who, at some level, as even the women who love them realize, are unreliable and undependable. But these men also possess enormous personal charm, the sort of charisma that makes them almost irresistible to certain women. These are men who radiate a central core of emotional anguish, who seem to conceal tragedy and drama. They may not write poetry, but they are nevertheless versions of the Byronic hero.

What makes these men so attractive? Even a casual reading of Byron's poetry reveals that the women he really loved were all unattainable. He loved them as long as he couldn't have them. Why, then, is his type so attractive to women who *are* available?

The women who love these men want to heal them. They believe that they alone among women can do so. They are attracted to these men because loving them is the ultimate victory over other women.

Loving these men demands a continuous outlay of tenderness from women. Their competition with other women is given the best possible disguise. Falling in love, they believe they suffer more than other women, give more, are more complete as women. Falling in love, these women continue to win Father from Mother. They *become* Mother, maternally tender and devoted to the man.

Winning Father from Mother, however, also means that somewhere along the line, these women lost Mother for themselves. The real attraction exerted on them by a man who seems to crave mothering is their own transformation into Mother.

When a grown-up woman gives mother love to a grown-up man, she mothers herself. She retrieves the mother she defeated long ago. But, like her mother, she usually finds herself abandoned. As most women learn, Byronic men stick around only as long as mother love doesn't ask for a return commitment.

For these women, winning Father from Mother feels like an addiction. However, they are not addicted to the man, although withdrawal after such an affair can be as painful as withdrawing from heroin. They are addicted to their craving to replace, in their own person, the mother they lost. When the affair breaks up, recuperation can be very slow, because so much more than a romantic relationship has been lost.

Freud himself, in the first case history he published, in 1905, described what happens to a daughter who wins the competition for her father.

Freud's analysis of Dora K. lasted only three months, but it is as rich in melodrama as any contemporary soap opera. Eighteen-year-old Dora was brought to see Freud—"handed over" to him, in his own words—by her father, because she was suffering from suicidal depression as well as from a raft of physical symptoms, including shortness of breath, partial paralysis, fainting spells, and loss of voice.

Freud realized, in an insight revolutionary for the time,

that Dora's symptoms were related directly to her family life. She was caught in a sordid net of relationships among her father, his mistress, and the mistress's husband.

Although Dora was her father's favorite child, even nursing him through an illness when she was only ten years old, now her father seemed to want her to accept his mistress's husband as her lover. That way everyone—obviously except Dora—would be happy.

Dora's symptoms, which Freud called hysteria, disrupted the misery the adults had created for her. Hysteria, which most women know about because when we get angry some man usually says, "You're getting hysterical," is a great stopper. A woman who is hysterical doesn't have to explain herself. Since she knows no one will listen to anything she has to say anyway, she uses her own health, both physical and emotional, to get what she wants.

But Freud failed to understand that the situation in Dora's family was simply a logical extension of the power alliances within all traditional families. Of course, most families do not condone the sort of misuse of power perpetrated by Dora's father, but in the traditional family fatherhood and power go together.

Like Dora's father, Freud was willing to believe that the blame for her illness really rested with Dora. He was able to ignore the fact that her father treated Dora as if she were his wife. Instead, in an almost casual remark, Freud blamed Dora's mother for making her husband unhappy. Dora's mother, Freud tells us, suffered from "housewife's psychosis," an obsessive concern with keeping her house clean.

Summing up the case, Freud concluded that Dora's real problem was her suppressed and unconscious homosexual attachment to her father's mistress. But, when he revealed this startling interpretation to Dora, she broke off treatment. The "truth" did not convince her, so she set herself free.

In December 1900, however, Dora did not have the feminist movement to confirm her suspicion that Freud was wrong, and wrong in a way that profoundly harmed her. Freud missed several significant points about Dora's situation. For one thing, he missed the distorted relationship between Dora and her father. Both participated, although a child's participation is necessarily far more innocent than an adult's.

While her father had been overly seductive, Dora had gloried in being the woman he chose. She won the competition with her mother. Freud believed Dora and her father when they reported that Dora's mother was a person of no importance in their lives—was a person of no importance in *anyone's* life, since all she thought about was cleaning her house.

Today, of course, it is easy to understand Dora's mother in her desire to keep her house clean. It is easy to understand that a woman forced to give up her husband to her daughter, and forced to lose her daughter to her husband, might obsessively concentrate on cleaning the rooms symbolizing the emotional house she was powerless to remedy.

Freud's critical mistake grew out of the fact that he considered Dora's family life both traditional and universal. He considered it "true," and therefore could not see that such a life supported a process separating women from each other.

Freud was not entirely wrong when he told Dora about her love for her father's mistress. Earlier, Dora had been very attached to her. But he didn't understand that Dora loved her father's mistress because Dora loved her mother.

Freud didn't understand that Dora had lost her mother, emotionally, because of the traditional relationships in her family.

What Freud really believed was that competition between women for a man is "natural"—inevitably part of female development and female life. However, there is nothing natural about the separation of mothers and daughters. Yet Freud was confirmed in his belief by the entire tradition of Western literature, all the books and stories focusing on romantic relationships, all implying that competition between women for men necessarily happens to all women. Freud's significant failure was a failure of perspective. The way he read life was through a narrowly focused lens, seeing women *only* in relation to men.

Had he widened his perspective to see Dora in relation to her mother as well as to her father, he might have seen that her dominant connection with *all* women was competition with them for men.

He might have seen that her illness was a form of competition with her father's mistress, as she once again attempted to wrest his love and attention away from another woman. And Freud might have seen that even deeper and more hidden than homosexuality, Dora felt that when she competed with a woman for a man, she acted out love *for the woman*—she felt connected to her.

Had Freud been able to expand his perspective on Dora's case, he might have understood what contemporary psychologists know about envy. They know that envy is a thwarted identification.

When women compete with each other for men, they, like Dora, respond to a *disconnection* between them. They are unable to be "sisters"—to identify with each other—when one woman has a man and one does not.

So the envy experienced by the woman without a man is the consequence of her failure to feel connected to the other woman. She is envious—and often outrageously angry as well as desperately lonely—not merely because she doesn't have a man. She also doesn't have a woman.

## WE HAVE MET THE "OTHER WOMAN" AND SHE IS US: ROMANTIC COMPETITION AND POWER

In her recent book on romantic passion, the psychoanalyst Ethel Person writes that love triangles are about power. When we think about Dora's case, and about the triangles created in our own love lives, we know that Person is correct. In our society, power is disguised as love.

But while love triangles are created by three people, each one does not occupy an angle equal in degree of power. For example, when Katharine and Linda talked about their husbands' ex-wives, each talked about the person who lacked power in the love triangle.

The rage, the hysteria, the sheer craziness often marking the behavior of women *out* of power in love triangles *is* the expression of their power—the only expression available to them.

Maya, forty-three, left her husband, Sam, four years ago. Most of her friends thought that her decision to leave her sixteen-year marriage was an act of courage. He was an attorney, financially affluent, tall and handsome. She was about to complete her graduate education and return to the workplace after ten years spent raising their two children.

Today Maya is a calm, attractive, very sane woman,

with a career she loves and two healthy, emotionally stable children she adores. But it was not always that way.

"I think I went crazy for a while after I left Sam," Maya recalled. "I felt stifled in the marriage, but once it was over, I panicked—the sheer, overwhelming terror of being alone in the world just drove me crazy. I picked on the kids, didn't see my friends; I was simply a mess. But the most awful part was my response to Sam's girlfriend."

Much to her surprise, only three weeks after separating from Sam, Maya made the discovery that she was the "powerless" member of a love triangle.

She hated it.

"I guess this was the most embarrassing moment of my entire life," she said, wincing at the memory. "But now I'm pleased it happened. If it hadn't, I don't know where I would be today. I was on the phone with Sam, upstairs in my house. This was about three months into our separation, when I was still sleeping with a night-light and having nightmares. I couldn't stand that he was seeing this other woman. She was someone we had known for years, as a couple. You know, she was the woman Sam would use to tease me about my not being sexy. She and her husband divorced about two months before we split up, she called Sam, and they connected.

"She and I had never been friends, but I certainly didn't dislike her. Now I was obsessed with her. I thought about her all the time. And I was murderously angry at Sam. I felt like he had betrayed me—even though I was the one who had left him.

"So, on this particular day, speaking to him on the phone, I lost control of myself completely. I screamed that I would kill him and her, using terrible obscene language— which I never use—and went on and on for at least twenty minutes. I don't know why he didn't hang up on me, except that he was as hooked into the triangle as I was.

"After I stopped talking—and crying—I came downstairs. That was a day the kids were at school, but for some reason or other, I had the day off. There, looking at me with such sympathy, was the woman who cleans my house. I think I almost fainted when I saw her; I had forgotten she was coming and she lets herself in. That moment, knowing that she heard me say all those horrible things to Sam, I thought I would just die.

"But the really wonderful part is what happened next. Instead of running out of the house, screaming with disgust as I really expected her to do, she made me a cup of tea, and told me all about *her* insanity when her husband left her for another woman.

"It was as much that she was taking care of me as what she told me about herself that allowed me to calm down. I know that I will be grateful to her forever. After that, it just got easier. She let me know that I wasn't such a terrible person, and knowing that let me think about Sam and Joan more clearly. I realized that at least some of my craziness was due to feeling so erased, so powerless in relation to them. I was also able to admit that what kept me feeling that way was *me*."

Maya was very lucky. There, in her own house, just when she needed her most, was another woman.

Women can give to each other what Maya received. They can give the critically necessary knowledge that they exist and that they are "good" people despite what seems to be "bad" behavior. They can give each other the understanding that they are "women," not just "other women."

When women find themselves in love triangles, particularly when they occupy the point created by a romance between the other two, they feel both powerless and erased. They scream and they have tantrums so that they can be seen and heard—by themselves as well as by the other two.

However, even the woman who forms part of the romantic couple can feel erased and powerless. Even the woman who apparently wins the competition for love needs "the other woman."

Women make a mistake about love. Trained to be feminine, many of us *feel* love when we allow ourselves to submit to a man. Despite the feminist movement, often we still believe we are in love when we feel that the man is stronger and better than we are, when we *want* to take up his ideas and interests.

In the filmmaker Rob Reiner's recent movie *When Harry Met Sally*, Sally proves to Harry that all men have been fooled, at one time or another, by a woman faking an orgasm. But Reiner misunderstood the reason why women sometimes, although not always, do that. Often, women do it because they love the man they want to please with evidence of his potency. As Simone de Beauvoir knew, a woman feels love when she surrenders to a man.

Competition between women for a man is the tie that binds women together in our society. It is our competition that gives us agency—the sense that what we do and what we say will have an effect on the world. Because women feel that loving a man means surrender of their willpower, their self-definition, and occasionally their self-respect, the "other woman" is a necessity. Having another woman around proves what most of us really know about love: that it is never a one-on-one relationship. Perhaps especially women who are successful in traditional love relationships know this.

For example, in the September 1989 issue of *Vanity Fair*

magazine, Kevin Sessums described the women married to the five members of the Rolling Stones rock band as "unreconstructed groupies." He said that when "Mick [Jagger] comes into the room, Jerry [Hall], despite her own astronomical wealth, beauty, and intelligence, jumps up."

And so do they all, these very feminine women who have managed to keep their men despite the legions of other women dying to take their places. The Rolling Stones' wives are very canny. Each has equipped herself with a "female support system," a female relative who more or less lives with her to provide the assistance, nurturing, and, most of all, *equality* that allows her to remain the woman her husband wants her to be. These wives know that despite great wealth and the envy of millions of women, they would be erased without another woman in their houses. Women who feel love when they surrender themselves *must* also feel a sense of personhood. It can come only from another woman.

Women who cannot afford the luxury of a live-in female support system depend on their female friends. As Carrie, forty-one, said, "Marriage is tough enough, but without my two good friends to talk to, life would be impossible. At least when we're together I feel like myself."

But other women, often those who feel most desperate about having a man in their lives, find themselves in love triangles.

Sometimes these are the single women who seem to fall in love only with married men. Often what these women think about "the wife" reveals that their competition has more to do with proving their own existence than with getting the man.

Marcy, forty, who went through four relationships with married men before she began to understand her compul-

sion, remembered, "I would spend hours and hours thinking about her, whichever 'her' it happened to be—much
more time, really, than I spent thinking about him. I would
compare myself to her in every possible way—our looks,
body size, clothing, cooking, sexuality. I even tried to prove
that I would be a better mother by talking to him about
how much I loved my niece. In fact, whenever I did anything, even taking out the garbage, in the back of my mind
was the thought that I did it better—more gracefully, more
efficiently, with less complaining—than she did."

Marcy wasn't able to understand why she was attracted
only to married men until she could see her relationship
with her lover in the context of her relationship with his
wife. "The last man—the man I'm now married to—
helped me. He was the first who left his wife for me. But
then I got really scared. I realized that I didn't know what
we would talk about if we didn't talk about her, and I was
very anxious about how good I would look to him when he
was no longer comparing me to her. I really believed that
without her, he wouldn't love me."

However, Marcy, like Maya, was lucky. "After living
with my husband for about two years, and getting therapy,
I began to be convinced that he loved me for my strengths,
not my weaknesses. He said all along that what attracted
him to me was my independence and self-sufficiency—I've
always worked and loved it—but somehow I never believed him. I think now that what I was doing was trying to
make myself just like his wife—what I imagined his wife
was like, what I imagined all wives were like, living to
please their husbands. When I was single, and competing
with her, I could despise her for that, but after we got
married, that's the way I thought wives should be."

In many marriages, the misconceptions Marcy suffered from fuel the marriage itself. These are relationships where husbands engage in a series of affairs, or sometimes mere flirtations with other women, and then "confess" their dalliance to their wives. In that love triangle, the marriage gains stability because the *wife's* existence depends on the "other woman."

## WHY CAN'T A WOMAN COMPETE LIKE A MAN?

When women compete with each other for men they compete *to be* possessions. When men compete with other men for a woman, they compete *to have* possessions.

Western literature undeniably is filled with portraits of men suffering, quite badly, from obsessive, jealous, rivalrous love for a woman. One has to think only of Vronsky's burning eyes as he gazes at the married Anna Karenina, or Swann, desperately, insanely in love with the coquette Odette.

As is the case for women, psychologists and writers understand this sort of obsessive love as "being in love with love," craving the ecstatic highs *and* the abysmal anguish that accompanies such relationships. But because these portraits have by and large been written by men, the fact that men love actively, that men deliberately, intentionally seek their obsessions, is obscured.

What men get when they possess an obsessive love is proof of their masculinity. What women get in order to prove their femininity is the opportunity to *be* an obsession. And there is no law regulating equal opportunity suffering.

When women define themselves as men's obsessions, we call them *femmes fatales*—fatally feminine women,

women who are so feminine that no man can resist them. Every woman knows about femmes fatales—they are the women our mothers warned us not to be.

Femmes fatales are grown-up versions of bad girls. They are dangerous to other women. They are created by men's fantasies, and they are the women men fantasize about.

But what happens to a femme fatale when she becomes obsessed with a man? What happens to a femme fatale when *she* wants a possession?

A good example of such a reversal is contained in the film *Fatal Attraction*. When *Fatal Attraction* was released, depicting an adulterous relationship between a husband and a femme fatale, wives would nudge their husbands during the movie and threaten severe penalties. They needn't have worried. By the end of the film, it is clear that the filmmaker has done to the femme fatale what all the wives in the audience would like to do. He has given her an obsession.

When a femme fatale falls in love, having an obsession makes her a witch. Her role is to be, not to do. When she becomes active, she must be punished.

Transforming her into a witch makes visible her outlaw status. Her life depends on masculine protection. Forfeiting that, she gets burned at the stake or, in the movie version, shot through the heart by the virtuous wife.

When a man takes a woman from another man, we call it theft. But men practice honor among thieves. Rarely will a man act with direct discourtesy toward the man who has "taken" his woman, dated his former girlfriend, or married his ex-wife.

Shelly, fifty-one, described the following incident with a mixture of humor and wry irony: "Jeff came downstairs one morning, after we'd been married about six months, to find Hank, my ex-husband, in the kitchen scrambling eggs for breakfast. Hank was there to pick up our kids, since it was his weekend with them. The two of them couldn't have been nicer to each other. In fact, when I came down, I found them all eating together, and *I* felt like the outsider. It was as though Hank was giving me to Jeff. I'm not sure if I was angrier at Jeff for accepting me, or at Hank, for his presumption."

But when a woman takes a man from another woman we call it murder. Rarely will a woman who loses a man fail to take direct action against the woman who wins. There is no honor among these thieves. When we compete with each other for a man, we are off the map of civilized behavior. There are no rules for us to follow because competition for a man exists only in the margins of the story our society tells about itself. In fact, because the stories about women competing for men are told about "bad" women, Cinderella's stepsisters every one, we expect women to hurt each other when they compete.

However, that is not quite an adequate explanation. If women certify each other's existence when they compete, why is their competition often so bloody, so downright frightening to both women? If women really need each other, why do they make such real and terrible efforts to wipe each other out?

In order to answer that question, first we need to think about why women don't, or won't, compete with men, why women aim their anger at the "other woman" instead of at the husbands and boyfriends genuinely to blame.

Although we are learning, with alacrity, that success in the professional workplace, and in public arenas generally, means that we must compete with men, most of us still feel enormous apprehension about doing so. Most of us still believe that when we compete with men we will be labeled "ball-busters," "castrators," or "bitches." There is still a real emotional distinction between a strong man and an aggressive woman.

The prohibition against women competing with men is deeply rooted in our society. Historically, women have not had the educational or professional opportunities to win a competition with men. Since women were by and large financially dependent on men, they learned not to bite the hand that fed them, at least not so that the man would notice.

Competition between men and women went underground. Women competed with men when they burned dinner—every night, when they became incompetent at easy tasks, like cleaning a house or sewing on a button, and when they became "frigid," forfeiting their own sexuality for the covert pleasure of revenge. Women learned that direct competition with men could be very dangerous, could mean poverty and emotional misery. The deck was stacked against them. If they acted with open aggression against men, they would be punished.

Unlike men, then, women learned unconsciously to separate their aggression from their erotic desires. They learned to confuse aggression with anxiety, while they mistook subordination for love. Men were not forced to make such a separation between the aggressive and erotic drives motivating them. For men, work and love can be fused. Men can be erotically stimulated by their work, while they are aggressively active in love.

Men can be *subjects* in work and in love, but when women learned to separate the erotic from the aggressive, they learned to be objects in love and subjects in aggression.

Diane, forty-five, a successful lawyer with a high-

powered corporate practice, offers a succinct example of
such separation. "I never could understand why, when I
would come home after a day of tough negotiating where I
didn't give an inch, I would be such a wimp with my
husband," she said. "My sense of myself, of who I am and
what I can do, seemed to vanish completely. It was like my
head suddenly filled with radio static—I literally could not
think clearly."

Like generations of women before her, despite her education and professional training, Diane still suffers from an
unconscious belief that women are not subjects in relation
to the men they love. Although she wishes it were otherwise, even in relation to her own husband Diane finds
herself acting like an object. She responds to him without
the aggression essential to self-definition, the aggression
that says "I am," "I want," and "I can think clearly about
who I am and what I want."

Historically prohibited from competing with men,
women have separated, emotionally and psychologically,
their feelings of selfhood from their romantic relationships
with men. Instead, they find their sense of self, their subjectivity, with other women.

Ironically, in one way, this split has given us women a
tremendous advantage over men. We have friends; most
adult men do not. We have female friends because we know
we need them. We drink coffee in each other's kitchens. We
make time in busy schedules for lunch and dinner. We
nurture our friendships with each other in order to confirm
our subjectivity. But while we offer each other support and
affirmation, the separation between the erotic and aggressive drives we have been trained to make exists even among
friends.

It is visible most clearly in the kinds of conversations we

have with and about each other. When women talk to each other they tell stories—which our society calls gossip. But women who are good friends know that all gossip is not equal.

When good friends tell each other stories about friends who are absent, they do so in order to continue the web of relationships in which they participate. They do so in order to create that web. Those stories, filled with the same details as more malicious gossip, are dominated by loving concern.

But when women tell stories about other women who are *not* their friends, whom they envy, with whom they cannot identify, they seek to destroy. As all women know, gossip can be destructive and terrible. Because we have been forced to separate our aggressive and our erotic drives in relation to men, we locate our aggression in our relations with other women.

While those relationships can be compassionate and fulfilling, they also can be genuinely terrifying. Especially for women concerned with being feminine—with being rather than doing—malicious gossip reflects their unconscious belief that when they are subjects, they hurt other women.

Since feminine women feel most like subjects with other women, other women are the people who seem to get hurt most frequently.

When we compete for men our behavior seems to confirm a statement written by a man: "All is fair in love and war." Competition in love *is* war for women. As in the guerrilla warfare it resembles, no holds are barred. We fight to preserve our homes and territory; we fight for existence. But we do not fight with men. Our battle is with other women.

We compete with each other because that's what men want us to do. Often these are the men we really know, not the abstract "man" representing patriarchy. They are the men we marry, the men we love. In our society, when we compete with each other we are diverted from competing with men. There is even an argument drawn from biology to reinforce women's competition—men are polygamous, women are monogamous.

But men are not the enemy, and many men, just like many women, suffer from the social assumptions made about their "nature." Men, like women, learned to relate to other people in the context of traditional family life, where ideals of mutuality often are overwhelmed by realities of dominance and subordination. And many men, just like many women, long for some way out of the mess we call love.

## COMPETITION IN MARRIAGE

Despite the social prohibitions forbidding women to compete with men, we do have an institution in our society that *ideally* should allow men and women to compete so that they could provide each other with an equal challenge to grow and develop. That institution is called marriage.

When women and men marry, they both hope to establish a genuinely mutual relationship. But all too often, the illusion that men and women don't compete reinforces a traditional imbalance of power in marriage that precludes mutuality.

Did you ever wonder why all the female-centered fairy tales, the stories about Cinderella, Snow White, and Sleeping Beauty, end with marriage? Or rather, these stories end when the prince and princess are at the point of marriage. Fairy tales do not reveal what happens after the wedding. That story is harder to tell, because it describes, necessarily, the competition between women and men.

Many women believe that after they marry the competition with other women will stop. To some degree, they are right. The competition aimed at making a woman into a wife does shift. It becomes a competition between women and men.

Women who are wives compete with their husbands. In fact, it's sometimes a relief when "another woman" intrudes on a highly conflictual marriage. Having an external enemy provides diversion from the real competition between spouses.

Sometimes we can even admit this relief. "Long after we divorced, at least four or five years," said Sara, forty-nine, "I realized that the fury I felt about Andy's girlfriend made life so much easier. Andy and I had been fighting for years, but we were careful not to cut each other up too badly. I never said the things I knew would make him leave, like insulting his sexual prowess or telling him he was a failure, and he never told me I was a horrible mother or that I looked ugly. We both saved that stuff as secret weapons, sort of the ultimate nuclear attack.

"But we both wanted out of the marriage," Sara continued. "We just couldn't let go. When I found out that he was seeing another woman, I felt like some dam had burst. I could say all the things I'd been holding back, and say them in a way that left me innocent. I could say that only a failure like him would choose a slut like her: things like that."

Years later Sara understood that her marriage had been destroyed by the hidden competition between her and her husband. She recognized that the "other woman" allowed her finally to compete with Andy out in the open. She understood that their secret competition had created a profound—and, in their case, irreparable—distrust between them.

"We never trusted each other enough to disagree," Sara said. "I felt that if I wanted something he didn't, I would have to change or adapt. But the fault is as much mine as his. Since I never believed he would give me what I wanted, just as my father only gave my mother what she *didn't* want, it was easier to transfer all that hostility onto Andy's girlfriend. In a certain way, I needed Andy's affair as much as he did."

Marriage, in our society, is based on a set of assumptions and expectations. Both men and women assume that monogamy is part of the contract. It is interesting, therefore, to realize that we have no infantile models for monogamy. Even our beloved mothers were not really faithful to us—they were involved in relationships with our fathers.

When infants discover this painful fact of social life, around the age of two or three months, their disappointment usually changes to real terror. They realize they are supposed to share the very person on whom their life depends.

When women marry, they often feel like the infants they once were. Their whole life is supposed to depend on this other person, and if he is not faithful to them, it can feel as if that life is very precarious indeed.

"I couldn't understand what was happening to me," said Eileen, thirty-two. "Here I'd been on my own since I graduated from college, but as soon as I married Bob I started worrying if he was even fifteen minutes late coming home. And not just worrying. I would work myself up into such a state that when he finally came in, usually only about ten minutes late because of traffic, I was a basket case."

Women are expected to give up much of their outside lives when they marry. Although contemporary women are more successful at maintaining professional identities than

were their mothers, they, too, respond to the social pressure
directing them to locate their primary emotional bonds
with their husbands and children.

Men, in contrast, are not equipped with quite the same
expectations when they marry. Men are supposed to support the household, not *be* it, so men expect their wives to
be monogamous, even if their own fidelity is not so rigidly
guarded. But for women, monogamy can extend far beyond sexual virtue. For women, monogamy in marriage
also means emotional fidelity. For women, fidelity means
noncompetition.

Historically, women, like men, often have confused self-
control with controlling other people. Many women, like
many men, have not learned that one can choose monogamy only for oneself. They have not learned that monogamy is a desire, a principle, and a cultural ideal, not a
fundamental law of nature. But unlike men, women have
not been able to institutionalize male monogamy through
legends, myths, novels, and inheritance laws. Women have
had to rely on the good faith of their husbands.

Moreover, with even more dangerous consequences for
women's characters, women have had to rely on secrecy
and deceit, on going through their husband's briefcase
when he's doing Saturday errands, on opening his mail, and
eavesdropping on his phone conversations.

Some women, having sad experience with male infidelity, learned to separate the men they marry from the men
they love. Believing that the only man who would be faithful was the man who loved you more than you loved him,
they paid for security with their own unhappiness.

When women compete openly with their husbands,
they often feel "unfaithful" and fear that their "infidelity"
gives the husbands permission to be unfaithful to them. So

women often try, unconsciously, to fail when they compete with their husbands. Like Diane's, their heads fill with "radio static," their voices rise when they ask simple questions such as "Whose turn is it to wash the dishes?" Sometimes, in fact, women convince themselves that there is no competition in their marriage at all.

Jeannette, forty-two, is a good example. Jeannette married for the second time when she was thirty-three. "I made a conscious decision that I wanted children and a family. I also felt secure enough about myself to know what I wanted because of my first marriage, when I was twenty-two. It only lasted a few years, but I learned a lot about myself, and a lot about what not to do again."

One of the most important things Jeannette won't do again, she said, was compete with her husband. "I'm a very competitive person, so this time I knew I wanted a man who was not competitive like my first husband. When I met Howard, I knew it would be OK because he's a scientist; he spends all his time in a lab and doesn't even know about the outside world, let alone care enough to compete in it."

Jeannette's clear-sighted appreciation of her own character sounded admirable. But her comment about her own competitiveness remained suspicious. Trained not to compete with men, women can easily be persuaded they are competing when they voice their desires or when they disagree.

Competitive people generally suffer from lowered self-esteem, and since Jeannette displayed real self-confidence, I asked her to tell me more about the small details of her marriage. For example, did she feel exploited, since she had taken leave from her profession in order to raise their two children?

Clearly, this was not the case. As an early-education

specialist, Jeannette, when she chose to stay home with her young children, acted on professional principles informing her thinking about what young children need from their parents.

And, as she quickly added, Howard gave her plenty of help in the house, doing all the grocery shopping and weekend cooking, although she did find herself resentful that when he spent time with the children they both called it "baby-sitting."

Still, the picture Jeannette offered of her marriage did not quite hang together. For instance, there was the issue of money. Jeannette continued to work part-time, but both she and Howard believed that her money was "extra."

"My money goes for the incidentals that we couldn't otherwise afford," Jeannette reported. "Even though literally fifty percent of it pays the sitter, I use the rest for buying Chinese food when I don't feel like cooking, and dinners with my friends, things like that."

Howard believed, she said, that she should pay the sitter since the sitter was necessary only because Jeannette wanted to work. And Chinese food and pizza were extravagances he was not prepared to support since he did the food shopping once a week, buying enough supplies for the five dinners Jeannette cooked.

"Howard's attitude is that this is something that benefits me, not something he wants. But, you know, when I think about it, all of his personal expenses come out of household money. I really pay for the things he doesn't agree with, things he can't even understand my wanting. Even a weekend away for the two of us comes out of my money, since he hates to travel."

Like Jeannette, women often work part-time in order to have enough money not to explain to their husbands why they want what they want. They work so that they won't have to compete for their desires. They work so that they won't have to disagree.

In traditional marriages, competition means imposing one's own perspective about the world on one's spouse. It means one partner, usually the wife, is unable to articulate her desires or sometimes even realize she disagrees with her husband.

Even as Jeannette told me that Howard was "not at all competitive," she realized that since they have been married he has done all the "holiday" cooking. "I'm a very good cook," she said; "I like to cook. Lately, though, I just cook for the kids. I appreciate Howard's pitching in, but the trouble is he never cooks anything he doesn't like to eat. How could I complain when he was working so hard? I guess that I miss the praise I used to get for my cooking. I always set the table, but nobody notices that. I also miss the traditional dinners. Howard won't eat meat, and we're Jewish. So on the High Holidays, when I would make a traditional brisket, we eat fish. It may be healthier, but I feel like I've lost a part of my childhood."

As is the case in many marriages functioning along lines of dominance and subordination, Howard and Jeannette concealed their competition by rationalization. She believed her self-confident, assertive personality had ruined her first marriage. She determined to be a "better" wife the second time around—being less competitive, or, in reality, confusing competition with disagreement. He, marrying an independent woman at a time when the feminist movement had demonstrated that men should help with parenting and household chores, believed he was pitching in.

Both were right and both were wrong. Behind their conscious rationalizations was a competition to be the per-

son who was right about life, a competition Jeannette was
losing.

When wives compete with their husbands, they can feel
both unfaithful and rebellious, but in all marriages, when
husbands and wives conceal their competition, both partners "agree" not to allow each other to grow and develop.
For both partners, the stability of the marriage depends on
an unchanging relationship. They compete to make each
other stay the same.

When husbands and wives compete to impose on each
other their ideas about how the world works, when they
compete to keep each other paralyzed, they regard each
other as possessions. They see their marriage as an invest-
ment, and they both suffer. Yet marriage traditionally has
offered women a way to feel special and superior to other
women, other women who are not married.

This kind of superiority has separated women from each
other. It is a superiority that vanishes quickly when a
woman is divorced. It has given married women a false
sense of self-esteem. It has made the "other woman" a
necessary component of the institution of marriage.

Elaine, thirty-eight, recently divorced after fifteen years
of marriage, said, "What I really hate about being single
again is that now I'm just like all the other single women I
sneered at when I was married. Now I feel just like one of
them, just another piece of meat on an overstocked mar-
ket." Single again, Elaine has become an "other woman."
But "other women" exist in direct proportion to the degree
of concealed competition between husbands and wives.
When a wife can't compete with her husband, she competes
with an "other woman."

## WINNING HIM CAN MEAN LOSING YOURSELF: THE DIALECTIC OF CONTROL

Like Elaine, when women compete for men we often feel we are all in the same degraded position, so we manipulate and exploit each other in ways we have come to associate with women competing for love. But when we do so, we lose one of the most important bases available for esteeming ourselves. We lose our capacity for empathy. Socialized to feel with other people, most of us like ourselves best when we are compassionate and sympathetic, and feel enhanced when our lives touch and are expanded by understanding another person. But when we compete for men, we stop trying to empathize with each other. Instead, we try to cancel each other out.

Ironically, trying to win a man, we imitate masculine behavior. We engage in cutthroat, no-holds-barred competition for survival, and experience a breakdown in the psychological and emotional process of recognition.

Our existence is confirmed when someone outside ourself recognizes us. That's why the first stages of a love relationship can feel so good. At last, we feel, someone really recognizes who we are. At the same time, there is no greater insult we can deliver than the failure to recognize another human being.

Edith Wharton wrote a short story, titled "Autre Temps...," about a woman whose divorce scandalized New York high society at the turn of the century. Her punishment, acutely terrible, is meted out to her by all the people she grew up with, who refuse to recognize her. They "cut" her, right out of their lives, and out of her own as well.

In competition with each other for men, women deny each other recognition. Instead of realizing that we use our competition to feel like subjects in our own lives, many of us believe that the "other woman" denies our own existence, even as we try to deny hers.

Lana, fifty-nine, described her response when she discovered that her husband was seeing another, much younger woman. "I felt so humiliated. They acted as if I didn't exist, didn't count in any real way. Joe's girlfriend was someone who had been to dinner, several times, at our house. How could she treat me that way?" Yet although Lana's marriage was far from happy, even though she wasn't sure she loved Joe, she felt, "If she gets him, I'm nothing."

The consequence of this breakdown in recognition is the bloody competition women know so well. When recognition fails, the desire to dominate takes over. But the woman who wins, dominating another woman, can lose herself.

Psychoanalyst Jessica Benjamin, in her book *The Bonds of Love* (page 53), calls it the "dialectic of control: if I completely control the other, then the other ceases to exist, and if the other completely controls me, then I cease to exist. A condition of our own independence is recognizing the other. True independence means sustaining the essential tension of these contradictory impulses; that is, both asserting the self and recognizing the other."

Thus, while winning the man can mean completely controlling the other woman, it also can mean losing oneself by annihilating the other woman who has confirmed one's own existence.

When women become aware of this dynamic, the results can be quite surprising. For example, Dina, forty-three, talked about her experience with "the other woman" in her twenty-three-year marriage. Unlike Lana, Dina had the unusual opportunity to discover exactly what she had lost.

"When I found out that Richard was seeing Colleen, I was beside myself with anger. In addition to everything else—the feelings of betrayal, of humiliation, of pain—I also was just flabbergasted that he would choose someone without any substance at all. Colleen was only about twenty-two, blond, blue-eyed; she didn't work. She was just a 'bimbo,' as far as I could tell.

"It turned out that Richard really wanted to stay in our marriage, but he wasn't able to end the affair immediately. He felt too guilty about Colleen, and he was scared, because she threatened all sorts of things, including suicide. Neither of us believed her, but there we were, caught in this awful mess.

"Colleen started calling us and hanging up at all hours of the day and night. It got worse and worse, and finally, I called her. We talked for two hours on the telephone. After that, while I was still very, very angry at Richard, I wasn't angry at Colleen. She had become real to me, and I had become real to her. I realized that she wasn't a bimbo, she was just like me, hurt and scared and out of control. After we talked, she was able to stop harassing us because she felt that she existed for me, and I existed for her.

"And I gradually got less angry and less obsessed, because talking to her also made me feel less out of control. Putting our marriage back together has been very slow work, but I don't think it would have happened at all if I had remained so angry at Colleen. I had to stop wanting to destroy her before I could even begin to see if anything was left between me and Richard."

## COMPETING THROUGH THE "TRUE SELF"

In order to "assert the self" while recognizing "the other," women need to feel a sense of authenticity, yet exactly such a sense is denied to them when they compete for a man. Competition for a man means that they inhabit roles—the roles of femininity.

Women in competition act out femme fatale, wounded wife, abandoned lover, tender mistress, devoted daughter, and the mother-you-never-had.

Often we forget that a real self exists. The roles we play are the roles we read about in novels, poems, fairy tales, and legends. They are the roles we see women enact on stage and screen. They are the roles that define what being a woman is all about. They are roles written for women by men.

When people are inauthentic in their behavior with each other, we call it "using" behavior. We frown on it. We disapprove of the people who manipulate and exploit others for their own ends. We know that they are people to distrust, to be wary of, to stay away from.

Yet most women think of each other in exactly that way. We fail to recognize that the other women competing with us for men share our desires and our fears. Instead, we see other women as exploiting men for their own purposes. We see that other women use *us* for their own desires. We see other women as fundamentally inauthentic. But we do not see ourselves. We are carefully taught not to identify with fairy-tale witches and soap-opera bitches.

D. W. Winnicott, who specialized in child psychiatry and contributed to the object-relations branch of psychoanalysis, thought in a different way about using people.

To Winnicott, using another person did not mean degrading or demeaning the other. It meant being able to benefit, creatively, from the other's existence. And in order to do so, it meant being certain that one's actions would not destroy the other person, that one's "badness" had limited power to harm—the other would survive.

Winnicott was concerned about the alienation and despair so prevalent in twentieth-century emotional life. He believed that such estrangement was derived from living with a "false self," which he contrasted to a "true self." Unlike the false self, the true self does not merely adapt and resign itself to its environment. The true self enhances and transforms reality with its own desires.

When we compete for men, we live with false selves. We resign ourselves to our attempts to annihilate other women. We use each other, and ourselves, improperly, manipulating and exploiting. We are as alienated from our own vitality and creativity as any of T. S. Eliot's "hollow men."

For example, Heidi, forty-eight, remembers that her first affair with a married man made her "feel like a monster." She said, "There was no place to turn to find out that our relationship was hardly unique. This was back at the beginning of the sixties, when the only books about affairs were novels about wicked women, like *Anna Karenina* and *Madame Bovary*. I was too ashamed to talk to my friends. I felt that being with Tom confirmed how awful I was."

When we compete for men, we believe we are "bad" people. The false self we live with, and through, teaches us that inside our deepest recesses lurks an evil witch. So we carefully restrict our self-awareness to the roles we are assigned by femininity. We convince ourselves that wrong is done to us, instead of admitting the wrong we do.

The evil witches we are told live inside us terrify us.

They are the "bogeymen" that our society uses to restrict women.

Often we are so frightened of what we believe to be our "natures" that we idealize our fathers and husbands in order to place a protective wedge between us and our own imagined destructiveness. Heidi, for example, whose affair confirmed her "badness" when she was only twenty-one, went on to live within an unhappy twenty-five-year marriage because as long as she was married she believed that she "was a good girl. I really felt," she said, "that being married saved me from hurting other women. You could say I was naive, but for most of that time I believed that if I was single, I would simply have one affair after another with married men. At the same time, part of what made me so unhappy while I was married was the constant fear that other women were after my husband. I just assumed they were as bad as I knew I was."

Instead, as Winnicott's work implies, we need to reconsider the way we compete for men. We need to recognize that all women who want men compete for them.

Recognizing our competition does not mean that we will suddenly love each other, or cease our attempts to take what another woman has, but it does mean that we can devise a set of rules where none presently exist.

Once we recognize both that we all do compete for men, and that doing so does not confirm our own evil, we can write our own story about what we're doing, instead of living the story men have written for us.

"I fell in love at first sight," said Dana, forty-four. "I realize that sounds ridiculous, like some trashy novel, but honestly, that's how I felt. That was five years ago, and I still love him. But I've never told him how I feel, and I don't obsess about him, because this love story is a little more complicated than usual.

"When we met, he was married. He still is. And he's happy with his wife, although I knew that he was very attracted to me. I knew that I had a real decision to make. I think if I had wanted to, I could have messed up his marriage. But I was lucky. I wasn't twenty when we met, and I knew that living with self-respect was at least as important as living with him. I knew that competing with his wife would be wrong because it would hurt me as much as it would hurt her."

Recognizing her desire to compete, Dana was also able to recognize herself. She did not allow herself to fall back on the old feminine strategy that disguises competition between women, the feeling that she was overwhelmed and swept away by love.

Instead, achieving self-control, Dana became self-empowered. "I'm a much stronger person than I was five years ago," she added. "I know that there are other men I can love because I love myself. I'm proud of myself. If I had gone after the man I loved, I would have destroyed myself, even if we had wound up together."

Although Dana's story seems to uphold a conventional version of marriage, wives, and other women, when Dana tells it she reveals quite another message. If the man she loved had been unhappily married, she might well have "gone after" him, and might well be living with him today.

Either way, Dana's own "happy ending" has more to do with her self-knowledge, self-respect, and self-control. What Dana reveals is that self-control doesn't necessarily mean noncompetition. It means *knowing* competition— and choosing what to do about it.

If we, like Dana, are to use our competition for men as a route to self-empowerment, we will have to give up the role of wretchedly martyred victim. This is very hard for most women, who have been socialized to believe that "good" women are victims.

But giving up the victim's role involves more than creating new definitions of how to be a woman. It involves admitting all sorts of new, and not necessarily pleasant, relationships into our lives. We will have to learn to live with our husbands' new wives; they will have to learn to live with us.

"When my husband married the woman he left me for, I was wild with anger," said Sheila, forty-seven. "I vowed I would never let her near my kids. I told them how horrible she was, and made them feel that seeing their father was betraying me. I'm not proud of all that.

"I finally began to think about my Aunt Hilda," Sheila continued. "When I was a kid, Aunt Hilda was the relative we hated to see come for a visit. She was the one who insisted that there's only one way to do things, and that's her way. But no one ever dreamed of kicking her out of the family. We might have wanted to, but we knew she was there for life.

"Thinking about Aunt Hilda, I realized that I was the one causing all the trouble, that it wasn't my husband's new wife who was making us miserable, it was me. And gradually, I realized that feeling like her victim was hurting me much more than it hurt her. I might not like her, but there she was, just like Aunt Hilda, part of the family."

We need to figure out how to be subjects in love—not simply with men, but more significantly, with ourselves. "I'm so tired of the war stories," said Terry, thirty-six. "I don't want to hear about how badly my friends are treated by men. I don't want to hear about what a jungle it is out there. I want to hear about their *lives*."

Although many women would reply that their lives *are* a jungle, Terry means that she wants to hear her friends talk about themselves actively, assertively, with more self-love and less self-pity. She wants to hear about a domesticated jungle, in the best sense of that word, a jungle made into a place where women can walk.

## ALONE, BUT NOT LONELY: COMPETITION AND DESIRE

What women have missed is that being in love has no connection with giving themselves away. Their competition for men is linked intricately to believing that love means some sort of subordination and surrender, while they reserve their active aggression for each other.

But a model for a competition that is a mutual challenge does exist in sexuality. The enormous emotional pleasure we experience in erotic union results from the tension between losing ourself in the other at the same time we are recognized as who we really are.

It is, as Jessica Benjamin writes in *The Bonds of Love* (page 29), the tension between "loss of self consciousness without the loss of awareness." When we are at our best, sensually and sexually, we are competing to take and to give pleasure.

But this is a new way for women to think about sexuality. Traditionally, female sexuality has been equated with the ability to attract. Women were supposed to be attractive rather than to exercise their desire. Yet being sexual at all means being aware of and in control of desire. Right now, we're not even sure what a desiring woman looks like if she doesn't resemble a witch or a bitch. The writer Alice Munro, describing in "Labor Day Dinner" a woman about to recognize her own sexuality, calls her "hesitant new grass."

A desiring woman is the story not yet written. Right now, we don't have any useful maps of the territory that will be discovered when two desiring subjects come together. Right now, we're making them up.

Women who desire are fully developed subjects in their own right, just like men. But many of us confuse the notion of subjectivity with the fear of loneliness. Socialized to identify ourselves in terms of our relationships with other people, many of us fear that being a subject means being solitary and emotionally isolated. Being a subject means being lonely.

Again, D. W. Winnicott's ideas point the way. Winnicott believed that a young child, around the age of eighteen months, needed to have her mother in the room in order for her to learn to play alone. Paradoxically, learning to be alone requires the knowledge that someone else is there.

When we grow up, of course, we expect our mothers *not* to be there. We expect that we will have internalized a version of a loving mother with whom we can comfort and nurture ourselves. However, many women experience being alone as desperate loneliness. Somewhere along the line, the mother inside, the mother present all the time and everywhere, has turned into an ugly old crone.

Instead of being able to play alone, then, many of us find ourselves competing for the man who will replace our lost inner sense of security. We compete for an idealized, magically protective father. Since without such an inner sense of security life can be quite terrifying, competition for men can be equally terrible.

But Winnicott knew that the inner sense of security was not exactly inside the self. He called it a "transitional area," between persons, a play space created by relationships that tell us that we are worth playing with. These are the relationships built on the knowledge that the other really is separate from, but at the same time connected to, us. These are relationships deep and rich in our understanding that our impulses will be tolerated, our destructiveness survived, and our creativity celebrated, genuinely mutual relationships where give and take wear the same face.

These relationships are playgrounds of growth and development, where the competition that says "I want" is also the recognition that you have the right to desire as well. When we compete with each other for men, we stop playing. The relationships we form, the roles we act, the costumes we wear become rigid and inflexible. The competitions we win or lose are the consequence of need, not desire.

When we compete for a man we are frightened—often scared stiff—that without him we will be alone. But feeling that way, we forget what Alison, forty-two, acknowledged: "I was much, much more lonely when I was married than now, when I'm divorced."

As all married women know well, marriage does not preclude loneliness. In fact, in marriage, women can feel much more desperately alone than they do when they actually live alone.

"The best thing that ever happened to me, although I certainly wouldn't have said so then, was having Jim leave me," said Marsha, fifty-two. "And the best piece of advice I ever received came from one of my good friends. She told me to collect soap. It was a joke, of course, but she was right. She meant that I should make a real effort to find some pleasure all my own. Soap was funny, but appropriate, because it's inexpensive and smells so good. I was terrified when Jim left, but gradually I discovered all sorts of possibilities I didn't know existed before. Including the possibility that I didn't *need* a man, I *wanted* him."

In order to transform our competition for men, women need to think about loneliness. We need to admit the reality that all of us, *some of the time*, are lonely. We need to cease believing in a magic marriage or romance to keep us safe from loneliness.

"I know the most important thing I've learned since my divorce was when I feel lonely and when I don't," said Anita, forty-nine. "When I was married, I thought that without my husband I would be lonely all the time. Now I know that while I do feel very lonely in the evenings, the mornings are just fine. I really don't want anyone around then, and I make sure that my evenings are occupied with friends or family. Knowing when I feel lonely allowed me to know what to do about it, instead of feeling that I would die from loneliness."

### AN EYE FOR AN EYE LEADS ONLY TO MORE BLINDNESS: COMPETITION AND RESPONSIBILITY

Things are changing in our society. We don't tell the old fairy stories so often, we don't believe that traditional families are the only families. We are willing, even eager, to discover new ways of loving each other. As family life changes in America, so will competition between women for men.

To a great degree, family life is changing because of the enormous numbers of women entering the professional workplace. Traditionally, children linked the mother with home, with holding and comforting. The father, in contrast, was active outside the house. He represented the world, large, mysterious, and exciting to the young child. Even the behaviors of mothers and fathers with young children express this division. Mothers cuddle; fathers toss children up in the air. Traditionally, women learned to compete with their holding, comforting mothers for love and attention from their exciting, stimulating fathers. This was very dangerous for daughters. Who would nurture and comfort them if they won the competition?

But now, with a new division of labor, mothers and fathers can be inside and outside the house. Both mother and father can represent the comfort of home and the excitement of the public world.

Girls and boys need both comfort *and* excitement to develop successfully. They need secure nurturing to allow them to explore the inner self and to develop self-love. They need the excitement of the outside world to stimulate curiosity and to create the sort of self-esteem connected with ability to act in public.

Having the mother and father inside and outside means that daughters will be able to identify with a new version of being a woman. A recent survey conducted by the *New York Times* indicates that this new definition is already occurring. According to the survey, women between the ages of eighteen and twenty-nine are far more optimistic about the combination of work and family life than even women slightly older, between twenty-nine and forty-four. Although these younger women have, by and large, not yet tried to balance a career with marriage and family, their optimism reveals a new sense of themselves, a new sense of strength they bring to the possibilities in their lives. When asked, these young women say they don't compete with other women for men. And for some, their words are not versions of the old noncompetition practiced by good girls.

Milena, twenty-three, expressed it well: "I definitely like having a guy around. If a man I like shows some interest in me, I respond, even if he's with another woman, as long as she's not a friend. I really expect that to happen in reverse. We don't own each other. But I'm careful not to try for a man who seems completely uninterested. And there are lots of ways to discourage a man, so I never have a problem with men who are seeing my close friends. I guess I have a set of priorities. Men are up at the top, but so are my friends and my work."

What makes Milena different from generations of women before her is her clear-sighted assessment of romantic life. She admits, without shame or embarrassment, that she wants a man in her life. At the same time, she does not feel humiliated or desperately lonely when she is without a romantic relationship. Unlike women in the generation before her, she doesn't feel that without a man she is a social pariah. She also wants other women and work in her life.

Milena does not overemphasize one element at the expense of the others, so when she competes for a man, she follows a set of rules that have never existed before. Her competition exists in a context of responsibility and trust— trust in herself and responsibility for other women.

And Milena's generation has absorbed yet another social change, one much more difficult to measure than the effect of dual career households on daughters.

Milena, like thousands of other young women, is the child of divorced parents. However, Milena was particularly lucky. "My parents were never awful to each other," she said. "There were some bad times when they first got divorced, when I was eleven—my mother cried for at least four months straight, and they both said some pretty terrible things about each other. But after that, they settled down. They both made an effort not to put me in the middle of their fight."

What really transformed Milena's development, though, was her mother's new sexual life. "After a couple of years, by the time I was thirteen, she was dating. Not a lot, but enough so that I knew she liked men. The funny thing was that while my parents were married, I never saw them touch or kiss each other. Now I was seeing my mother kiss men. At first I suppose I was jealous, but that went away pretty quickly, because my mother was so sensitive about me."

Traditional wisdom directly contradicts Milena's experience. According to the usual way of thinking, Milena's sexual development should have been paralyzed when her mother began to demonstrate that she, too, was a sensual woman. Instead, Milena gained a comprehension of female empowerment and of female subjectivity. "When my mother remarried, when I was sixteen, I was delighted. I felt that she was doing something she had chosen, that marriage and sexuality could be a woman's choice."

Of course, Milena was exceptionally fortunate to have a mother who combined an appreciation of her own sexuality with the desire to take very good care of her daughter. She gave Milena the knowledge that life is multiple, that life contains many people to love. But she also gave Milena the knowledge that women are sexual subjects, that good women are sexy women. And revealing her sexuality diminished, rather than heightened, the sexual competition between mother and daughter. Now that she was certain of her own sexuality, Milena's mother could welcome and celebrate her daughter's sexual development.

Years after her parents divorced, Milena discovered that her father had left for another woman. But after a period of grief, Milena's mother did not allow herself to become locked in angry, bitter resentment. Asserting her own sexuality decreased her anger, both at the other woman and at her husband. She became present and accounted for, *to herself*, in her own life. She no longer needed the other woman, or her ex-husband, to tell her she existed.

Contemporary mothers have the historical opportunity to make their daughters subjects. Their own lives can be models for their daughters. They can be the strong women who produce other strong women.

Strong people compete with each other for what they want, but strong people also recognize each other's power. Their competition becomes a form of disagreement, a way to admit each other's desires. It becomes a way to figure out how to see the world as containing enough goods to satisfy everyone.

When women compete for men, they behave as if there is only *one* man around. Instead, women need to recognize what always has been true: that their lives are filled with relationships, many of which are important and significant. This is very hard to do in a society that insistently, in every possible way, tells us that the only relationship that counts is the one between a man and a woman.

But it's time for women to admit that romance always has depended on more than two people. Sometimes the "other woman" looks like an intruder; sometimes she looks like our best friend. But she's never been an accident—she's been a necessity.

*      *      *

We need to reconsider the old myths and fairy tales, the ones that teach women how to compete with each other. For instance, there is Psyche, the girl whom everyone revered for her extraordinary beauty.

Nevertheless, Psyche felt dead. She was a sexual fantasy for every man who saw her, and a sexual threat to every woman, but she had no life of her own. Only after the wind carried her away could she recognize Eros, her lover. Only when she was no longer the object of everyone's desire could she act on, or even know about, her own desire.

Psyche felt dead when she did not compete. She felt dead when every woman she met competed with her.

Reconsidering Psyche's myth, we see that the other women competing with Psyche actually were more fortunate than she. They were active, they felt alive, even if miserable; she was passive, dead to herself. And her beauty, despite what women have been taught, did not nearly compensate for her lost vitality.

What Psyche lacked was a female community. Her beauty, defined by men as the only important thing about her, isolated her from the women who accepted the patriarchal idea that a beautiful woman is especially privileged—she wins the competition. Competing with Psyche, the women around her found each other. Like Cinderella's stepsisters, they lived in a community defined by their competition. But because their competition for men was defined *by* men, they couldn't see each other. What we have to learn when we compete for men is what Margaret Atwood wrote in *Cat's Eye*: "An eye for an eye leads only to more blindness."

In order to play the game of love well, we need all the sight we can manage.

# *Chapter*

# 4

# *Competition at Work*

Helen, forty-five, is a dark-eyed, soft-spoken, slender woman. She conveys an impression of reliability. It is easy to trust her. She appears to be exactly what she is: intelligent, responsible, with an emotional warmth concealed beneath an appealing shyness. Most people like her. Most of the time, she likes herself.

But not right now.

"Oh, I can tell you about competition between women at work, all right. Oh, can I tell you!" she exclaimed.

"I still have nightmares, and this happened more than a year ago. Sometimes I think that I'm in worse shape than people who survive plane crashes. I can't seem to let go, not of my anger, and not of the pain. And deep inside, I guess I really believe that somehow I was to blame."

Although Helen begins speaking with real vigor, her anger deepening the color in her cheeks and lighting fire in her eyes, within seconds her body is sagging against the refrigerator of the friend's kitchen in which we meet. Her face, so recently pink with feeling, is now pale and sallow, her mouth trembling, her eyes downcast. Her pain is communicated so vividly that I can feel my own shoulders bend forward, my stomach clutch and grind.

Helen is talking about losing her job. Nearly eighteen months ago she was in a tenure-track position at a small private university. She had just published a book with a major university press; she was a huge success in the classroom; she was popular with her colleagues.

She was, she believed, certain to win a permanent position in the career she loved.

"I can't tell you how shocked and hurt I was when the vote came down negative," Helen said. "At first all I could think about was betrayal, and who exactly had done it. Then I realized that the 'no' vote meant I wouldn't be teaching anymore, and I got really depressed.

"But the worst part, the part I see in my horrible dreams, is that I was done in by *women*, people I thought were my friends. That seems to make it all so much worse, because I can't get over feeling that if other women would do this to me, I must have done something terrible to deserve it. I must have let them down in some way. But I can't figure out how."

Helen's experience is not unique. Her feelings of devastation, betrayal, and emotional mutilation were echoed by many of the nearly fifty women with whom I talked about competition between women at work. Although many of these women were able to recuperate faster than Helen, most retained the scars of shattered self-confidence Helen displayed. *All* felt, like Helen, that because they were "done in" by other women, they must, somehow, shoulder the blame.

After listening to Helen's story, I concluded that, indeed, she was *not* to blame. Her story fell into an all-too-familiar pattern, so familiar that it appears regularly as the basis for television programs.

Helen was caught in the right place at the wrong time. As many people discover who work within large and small institutions—academic, corporate, public and private sector—often political context counts more than personal merit.

As Helen talked, it became clear that her negative tenure decision had more to do with the prevailing winds of political alliances among her colleagues than with her own performance inside or outside the classroom. Although I was able quite easily to absolve Helen of any personal blame, *she* was not able to clear herself. Instead she suffered, and suffered severely, because her particular competitive loss reflects a new moment in our society: competition between women is out in the open. We are discovering that it is impossible to conceal our competition in the professional workplace. But we still take it very personally, and most of us still want to hide our competitive desires, mainly from ourselves.

Helen suffered because, in our society, we have no models for women who work together. Instead, we still use models drawn from family life. Helen found it easier— more comfortable emotionally, despite the enormous pain it produced—to believe that the women she worked with would not harm her unless she had hurt them first. Although she knew very well that women hurt each other in private life, she had staked her identity—both personal and professional—on the assumption that women would support each other in professional life. Helen, like many of us in her position, felt like a daughter betrayed by her mother, and like a good daughter, she found it impossible to accept that betrayal unless she could find a way to blame herself. As long as she blamed herself, she maintained an emotional connection with the women who did her in. She did not allow her "mothers" to abandon her. She gave up her self-esteem so she would not have to give up female support.

Like Helen, in the absence of models teaching women how to deal with professional power, we are using the new open and personal competition between us to figure out who we are at work—to decide whether we are mothers, daughters, friends, "the other woman," or men.

In today's world, we live with several myths about work. We believe that individual effort and individual merit count. We think that if we work hard, we can get ahead. We believe that work benefits the body and the soul, that it provides significance and meaning in our lives. At the same time, we know that the marketplace is tough and ruthless, that only the fittest survive. The pie is limited, and if your piece is larger, mine will be smaller. Big fish eat little fish.

These myths, which contradict each other, leave us with distorted relationships. On one hand, we are told that work is both a necessity and a good, that working makes us "better" people, and that success at work makes us happy. On the other hand, we are told that in order to be successful and therefore happy, we will have to make other people unsuccessful and unhappy. There simply is not enough to go around.

\* \* \*

Men as well as women suffer from the contradictory myths governing the workplace.

In *Modern Madness: The Emotional Fallout of Success*, psychoanalyst Douglas LaBier concluded, after making a seven-year study of life in the corporate workplace, that the most successful men he encountered, in terms of their powerful positions, were also the most emotionally ill. LaBier realized that his successful subjects had adapted to a work environment that applauded manipulative, exploitive behaviors. They had formed themselves in the image of a marketplace rewarding what could be described in psychological terms as sadism, and in political terms as authoritarianism.

LaBier also discovered that, in contrast, people who felt anxious at work, whose success was experienced as loss, were much healthier emotionally. In effect, the very anxieties these people suffered from actually certified their mental and emotional wellbeing.

They were suffering, LaBier concluded, from a perversion of values in the workplace, a distortion so profound and extensive that most of his "healthy" subjects blamed themselves for being unable to enjoy the fruits of their labor. They sought help from psychiatrists; they wanted to be "cured" so that they could better fit in. In other words, they were experiencing an anxiety all too familiar to most working women, one caused by blaming themselves for malignant conditions created by their environment.

However, here's a special twist for women: we blame ourselves in order *to excuse the workplace for not allowing us to fit in.* By doing so, we cling to a set of virtues developed for women in private life, like fairness, connectedness, compassion, generosity, and individual loyalty:

values established for people who do not have power over other people.

Judith Briles includes several dozen stories about women competing with each other at work in her recent book *Woman to Woman: From Sabotage to Support.* In each anecdote, women talk about financial loss, personal humiliation, emotional devastation, and shattered self-esteem. The dominant theme they voice is "What did I do to deserve such treatment? I was doing the best job I could." Each storyteller implies that the only reason she can think of to explain the terrible events that befell her is that she naively placed her trust in another woman.

In each story, what confuses the teller most is that the values she brought to the workplace turned out to be exactly the weaknesses her antagonist used against her. The storytellers in Briles's book are Cinderellas, every one, good girls who bring to their careers traditional good-girl virtues, like patience, endurance, tact, and sensitivity to others.

They paid attention to their work. In fact, they paid such close attention that they failed to hear the other message surrounding them—that although good girls are rewarded in fairy tales, they are punished at work.

The Cinderella women who tell the stories about competition with other women at work reveal their sense of powerlessness.

When, like Helen, they wind up blaming themselves, they demonstrate that they have internalized the misogynistic attitudes toward women that are prevalent in the workplace. At the same time, the successful working women we assume should have voice because they do possess power are carefully silent. Right now, in the stories women tell about competition with each other at work, silence signals power, not victimization.

This isn't really a new development for women. We have always talked more about our powerlessness than about our power. Traditionally, women bond with each other by sharing bad news. Just as we learned to compete with each other negatively in the domestic arena—telling each other how lacking our lives were—at work it is the women who *lose* who speak.

For women, even the contradictory myths men live by are not much good. No matter if women supervise other women, or work for them, all are confused. To all, competition feels like loss. For all, competition with each other implies failure. At the crux of the despair we experience competing with each other at work lies the absence of social ideals and myths to act as guides for working women. Where are the models for powerful women?

## WOMEN AT WORK ARE INVISIBLE WOMEN

By October 1984, fifty million American women were working full-time outside their homes. Statistics indicate that 90 percent of the girls now entering young adulthood will also enter the labor force.

Most of these girls will have no models with whom to identify. They will be the generation that makes up the stories about what happens when large numbers of women take their ambitions seriously and are as passionate about their work as they have been taught to be about their families and romantic relationships.

For most women, the struggle, even today, is enormous. Eighty percent of all the women who work outside their homes in this country hold the lowest-paid, most dead-end jobs. They work in factories, in shops, in other women's houses. When they come home after a nine- or ten-hour day washing other women's hair in beauty salons, they labor for another five or six hours cleaning their own homes and taking care of their own children.

Yet historically, even the lucky women have been complicitous about their own invisibility. They have helped foster a very powerful lie about women's work: the lie that their success at it *depends* on their invisibility.

"You know," said Elissa, forty-four, "it's only now that I have a house and family of my own that I realize how hard my mother worked all those years we were growing up. We come from the South, where women make houses beautiful. There were always fresh flowers around, and the house just sparkled. But my mother never complained—we really never knew that all that comfort depended on her. In fact, in a funny way, she would have been offended by our gratitude. We weren't supposed to know how hard she worked. Her work was supposed to be done gracefully, which meant that the house should seem to run itself."

Ideals of grace and elegance interfere with visibility. They coincide with another lie: that women who complain or ask for recognition are shrews.

So the lucky women made sure their work was secret, but they kept the secret of their labor-intensive days best from themselves. They complied with the larger social lie that women's work was easily done and painlessly accomplished. Instead, women learned to link recognition with qualities of the self, with generosity, loving concern, and emotional warmth.

Although these qualities are virtues, they nevertheless all involve women in a critical duplicity. Women were trained to understand that their labor was less serious than men's, to see their ambition as unfeminine. They were taught to work hard and deny that they did so.

By and large, contemporary professional women are the daughters of mothers who made their work invisible. They labor with a peculiar inheritance, which produces real emotional conflict in them. As the psychoanalyst Jean Baker Miller remarks, even when women do the same work as men, they tend to think of it as less "important."

As long as our society assumed that most women worked at home—itself a myth—it also assumed that women did not compare their work. Yet we only have to think about the television programs made in the 1950s to remember the stereotyped "kaffeeklatsches" women at home substituted for morning coffee breaks.

When women got together in each other's kitchens, they talked about their work. They talked about how difficult it was to be a wife and how complicated it was to be a mother. They traded recipes and tips for making their household work easier or more efficient. And they competed with each other—negatively and indirectly—about whose house was cleaner, whose children were more successful, whose food was more delicious, and whose husband earned the most money. But keeping their competition secret left women with a legacy of troubled relationships with each other.

"In the fifties, women weren't much good for each other," said Rose, sixty-eight. "I can remember when joining a women's group would have been unthinkable, something to be ashamed of." Competing secretly also meant that women learned to distrust each other, and to compete negatively, to say "Poor me," to say "I'm so fat; my kids are running wild; my house is a mess."

It meant that women's self-esteem came to depend on *not* working and *not* competing, and that their self-definition was fundamentally negative.

## CAN WOMEN BE "WOMEN" AT WORK?

Jean Baker Miller writes that women are socialized to develop a "self-in-relation." Our fundamental self-definition depends on a sense of connectedness to the other people with whom we live and work. Most women, in fact, find satisfaction in any activity that enhances and deepens the emotional connection between themselves and other people. Women have been taught to find personal satisfaction in the empowerment of others.

But our society has devalued and disparaged this "self-in-relation." Women's capacities for empathy, compassion, and generosity directly conflict with traditional cultural assumptions linking maturity to independence and individuality.

Marketplace values, focused on "the bottom line," extend and perpetuate this system that devalues women's "self-in-relation." They make it very difficult for a woman to be a "woman" at work. Instead, the professional workplace confirms a masculine model. The psychoanalyst and social theorist Michael Maccoby, author of *The Gamesman*, explains in his book *The Leader* (page 16), "It is at work that men have traditionally affirmed their values and found a sense of meaning, identity, self-esteem, competence, confidence, success, or failure."

What men affirm when they work is the sense of themselves as individuals. Their very identity depends on their separation from other people. Marketplace values are made in their image.

When men compete at work, they strive to achieve an ideal that inherently demands competition between them. Women, in contrast, are at a real disadvantage in a workplace constructed to support and foster individual effort and competitive striving, since we value affiliation. Although we experience competition as disrupting our connection with other people and feel it as a loss of self as well as a loss of community, in the workplace, individual development and success proceed only through competition. For women, it's a catch-22.

Maccoby writes in *Why Work?* (page 52) that "the strongest universal motivators to work are self-expression, hope, and fear." But for women, Maccoby's motivators produce enormous conflict. Self-expression, for example, depends on having a self to express. Maccoby, whose work on social issues demonstrates his liberal and humane ideas about human development, nevertheless omits the history women bring to work. For women, even a quality as necessary and fundamental to human life as self-expression is a problem. And being serious about our work means that failure is as serious as success. But women connect failure at work with failure experienced at home, where criticism usually is followed by emotional penalties, like withdrawal of affection, or even abandonment. Unlike men, women often play an *emotional* zero-sum game at work—one loss makes us feel as if *we* are lost.

Women want to succeed at work, but hope, like fear, is confused with emotional relationships. Traditionally, women have confused success with winning the approval of the people with whom they live and work.

Although work is usually conducted *among* other people, and success at work involves recognition *from* other people, work itself is conducted in relation to our own abilities; it is a relationship between the self and the task, and passion motivates our response to the job at hand.

This passion is linked to issues that bring up enormous emotional conflicts in most women. It means that we are fundamentally alone, that excellence is located in a challenge to the self, not in a relationship with another person. Since we define ourselves through a "self-in-relation," the challenge to excellence can be experienced as isolation, as being cut off from ourself rather than as self-enhancement.

Passion for our work means that we recognize our ambition and desire for power. Excellence means power and the ambition to attain it, yet most women experience power and ambition as disrupting relationships.

Traditionally, power has been a sticky issue for women. Defined in the context of individual achievement, power has meant winning while others lose, and having power has been experienced as being "selfish."

Generally, women with power have concealed it, becoming the women "behind the throne." For example, when the filmmaker Woody Allen offers us his portraits of the stereotyped Jewish mother, he fails to consider that his Jewish mothers practice power like good girls. They've learned that their desire for power must be concealed and can be exercised only when it's disguised as nurturing. Allen's Jewish mothers are as unhappy as their suffocated children, because they are equally bound in a relationship that confuses the power of achievement with the power of manipulation.

When women work outside their homes, their desire for power makes them "bitches," so powerful women often become the "office martyrs," overwhelming themselves with work in order to disguise their authority and power. The female boss manipulating and exploiting her secretary in the recent film *Working Girl* represents our society's real mythos of a powerful woman.

Nevertheless, women are writing a new chapter in our history. As they enter the professional workplace in ever larger numbers, they are creating new answers to questions about power, ambition, and passion at and for work, and building a relationship with work never before articulated by women in our society.

Women are writing a new history of women working—and competing—together.

## PROBLEMS OF AMBITION AND LEADERSHIP IN COMPETITION AT WORK

"I find that the other women at my office are much more important to me than the men," said Trudy, thirty-six, who occupies a midlevel position in a large management consulting firm.

"I don't mean all the women, of course," she continued, "just the women who are above me in the corporate structure. I've discovered that I'm fascinated to the point of obsession by them—how they work, what they wear, what their lives are like outside the office. I guess I'm desperate for clues about their success. I feel as if the more I know about them, the better chance I have to succeed also."

Contemporary working women like Trudy *are* passionate and seriously ambitious about their work. However, many working women experience their passion and ambition as a desperation provoked by feeling that they are in competition with the other women with whom they work. Some of this desperation, of course, is derived from the historical prohibition against women competing with men. Traditionally, women could compete *only* with each other. Competing with men was far too dangerous, often penalized by real failure and isolation as well as devastating misery.

The notion of the "glass ceiling" reveals that this prohibition still exists in very powerful and real ways within the professional workplace. Subliminally, women respond to the message that the path to success lies through another woman's—not a man's—job.

Historically, women were forced to compete with each other, but we did so mainly in domestic arenas, locating our competition between mothers and daughters, between wives and "other women."

Competing at home, we learned that if our competition was obvious, other women would abandon us. We learned to compete in ways designed to elicit support and reassurance from precisely the other women with whom we were competing.

We learned to deny our own ambitions. We discovered that our ambition provoked envy from other women, and we identified that envy with the resentment we sensed our mothers felt for and hid from us. We believed that if another woman knew what we had, she would take it away.

"All the time I was growing up," said Rebecca, forty-four, "I felt that I had to be very careful about telling my mother about any particular success. I know that she didn't consciously set out to tear me down, but inevitably, she would find a way to tell me that what I was doing was wrong, or stupid in some way I hadn't realized.

"Even when I was pregnant with my first child, for example, she managed to comment that she was surprised about the pregnancy since I never follow through on anything. She said this despite the fact that by the time I started having children, I had finished graduate school with two degrees. I now realize that even though she really wanted me to have children, when I finally did, it must have seemed to her that I had too much, a career *and* a family.

"I'm really careful even today, about revealing my ambition to the women I work with. I still feel that somehow I'll get hurt if they find out. And frequently when I feel ambitious at work, I also feel desperate. I want to get what I want *quickly*, before the other woman who wants the same thing moves in. I think I'm competitive in an impulsive way that does me more harm than good because I still believe I'd better take what I want before my mother finds out."

Competing in domestic arenas, we learned to mistake self-absorption for self-esteem. Even more important, we learned that what we achieved was connected, inevitably, to what other women achieved. In Saul Bellow's phrase, women learned to be eternal "contrast gainers." Feeling ourselves as failures, we measured ourselves through a comparison to another woman's even greater failure. And we learned to translate our desire for success into feelings of desperation, provoking us to compete in ways that genuinely hurt ourselves and our competitors.

"This is a rather bizarre story," said Jane, forty-one. "I feel somewhat uncomfortable telling it because I'm not sure I really want to learn what it teaches me. About four years ago, I was up for a promotion at the university where I teach, both in the English and women's studies departments. I was very open about my ambition. I have a real talent for coalition building, which I thought I could put to good use if I became director of women's studies. I also thought that the other women who worked with me—we were all feminists—supported me."

Jane paused, with a confused look on her face. "Even

now, four years later, I still feel that the parts don't add up to the whole. What happened was that far from supporting me, it turned out that the women I thought were my 'sisters' were actively working against me. I lost the position to a woman I didn't even know *wanted* the job. In fact, when I had talked to her, she said she was supporting *me*.

"Now I know that I was tremendously naive. I should have realized that being so openly ambitious was experienced by my colleagues as very threatening. The woman who did get the job was far more careful about concealing her ambition."

Jane's story is not simply about the sort of back stabbing that we associate with competition in the workplace, nor is she describing what sounds like a stereotyped version of how women behave with each other. Her story reveals a far more complicated dynamic, linked to the way women experience their own and other women's ambition.

Even among avowed feminists, the ambitions of one woman can be felt as disrupting sisterhood. When they acted against her, Jane's colleagues believed they were safeguarding, rather than destroying, the feminist community in which they participated. The competition Jane experienced is linked to the fact that women suffer from an absence of female leaders.

Jane wanted to be a leader. She wanted to possess the sort of power bestowed by group consent and the public acknowledgment that her talents and abilities would benefit the group. But for women, even those who define themselves as feminists, leadership is often confused with individual striving. When most women think of their talents, they think of their capacity to support and nurture other people, not to act as models for them. When they meet another woman who chooses to lead rather than to follow, they identify her as destroying the group instead of attempting to make the group coalesce.

Like Jane, many women who possess real leadership ability have experienced attempts by other women to make them return to positions within the group.

Donna, forty-six, is a good example. Donna formed her own law firm eight years ago, deciding that she would keep it small, hiring, in the main, female lawyers.

"I wanted to support the development of women in the profession," Donna said. "And for the most part, it's worked out very well. The vision I began with has become a reality, and the firm is quite successful.

"But," she continued, "I find that with increasing frequency, my time is devoted to hand-holding activities. Although the women I hire are competent and good at their work, more and more I find that they ask me for help with problems I know they can solve themselves. It's getting so bad that I hardly have time for my own work."

Donna's experience is common to women in positions of leadership. When her employees seek her assistance, what they also do is compete with her for her time. The more they get, the less she will have. The more of that time they get, the less she will be able to act as a model for them by doing her own work, and the more she will be "one of them."

Yet because hand-holding makes us feel good about ourselves, because we do it well and because most of us genuinely want to support the development of other people, we contribute to our own derailment. Since the women who lead have few female models themselves with whom to identify, the conflict between nurturing and leadership, and between group and self-loyalty, can be very difficult to resolve.

When Jane said her story was "bizarre," she really meant that because she wanted to lead, she feared she had betrayed her colleagues well before they turned against her. Jane felt guilty, though she knew that the best use she could make of her talents was *as* a leader. Revealing her own ambition made her feel as if she had failed to participate in a women's community.

This guilt—a socialized response to stepping out of the "good girl" persona—reflects one of the reasons why we have such difficulty both finding and keeping female mentors in our professional lives. Senior women, whether they accept the fact or not, are seen by younger women as leaders. Still, often senior women possess internalized evaluations of working women made by men. Although they have power, they *feel* powerless, often particularly in their ability to support younger women. They compete with younger women for a position they in fact already possess.

At the same time, younger women, like senior women, bring to the notion of female leadership a real distrust. While younger women know they need mentors, they are not certain they can trust a woman who has achieved some measure of professional success. They compete to bring her back to their level, instead of appreciating what she can do for them by using her senior status. Leaders or followers, the problem women acutely experience at work is that their workplace models are drawn from family life.

In the absence of a general professional identity, women transfer to relationships at work what they learned in their families about competition. Senior women have inherited the mother position for a whole generation of working daughters, yet these same senior women do not themselves have models for a new version of professional motherhood. They are making it up as they go along. And, as every mother knows, sometimes you get it right, and sometimes you get it wrong.

In turn, younger women often bring to their professional relationships with older women all the baggage they accumulated with their biological mothers. And, as every daughter knows, it is far easier to tell your mother what she is doing wrong than to appreciate what she is doing right.

In addition, some women, older and younger, feel real emotional distress at the notion that they may surpass their mothers. Success and ambition are bound up with being as good as, but not better than, their mothers. Ironically, failure at work can signal emotional success for women locked into this sort of relationship with their mothers. By failing, they remain successfully connected.

Often the consequences of this dilemma are acted out unconsciously, producing genuine pain for both senior and younger women. Jean, fifty-six, described her disappointment when Karen, thirty-two, left the law firm where they both practiced.

"When Karen joined us, I was very much aware of my responsibility as her mentor," said Jean. "I watched her, and helped her grow and develop professionally. When she decided to take a position with a large firm, I was really pleased at her success. But she left without so much as saying good-bye. She wouldn't even allow me to take her out to dinner to celebrate."

From Karen's point of view, however, her abrupt departure was an attempt to take care of Jean. "I knew that Jean wanted to leave our firm, and my new position was one for which she had tried several years ago. I felt that focusing too much attention on a celebration would emphasize my success and her failure," Karen said.

Jean and Karen were unable to communicate their complicated feelings about Karen's success. While Jean was genuinely pleased that her mentoring had assisted Karen, she also was conflicted about her own stagnation, highlighted by Karen's rapid rise. For her part, Karen, desiring to take care of Jean, ended by hurting her. Like Jean, she denied the unconscious strata of her actions and was unable to confront the competitive feelings she brought to their relationship.

Often when young women surpass their mentors, they treat them with what looks like casual dismissal. They are attempting to resolve their emotional dilemma by leaving "Mother" before she can leave them, the response they fear "Mother" will make to their successful competition.

Both older and younger women in the workplace need to construct new models for working women.

They need to figure out how to use their ambition and desire for power affirmatively, as a challenge to self and other, and as a way to enhance rather than destroy their "self-in-relation." They need to learn how to communicate—and compete—with each other beyond family models.

## COMPETITION AND COMMUNICATION

When we tell stories about losing competitions with other women at work, most of us fall into the category of "received knowers." As defined by Mary Field Belenky and her colleagues in their recent study, *Women's Ways of Knowing*, "received knowers" get their information from the authorities in their lives. They listen to outside voices, and assume that if they do what they are told, they will be rewarded. When we are "received knowers," we equate truth with states of feeling. We formulate rules for our behavior by making statements like "It makes me feel sick to compete with other women" and "Everyone knows you don't compete with other women." We don't form opinions of our own.

Received knowers are good girls. They have a difficult time when they find themselves in situations where hard work and good behavior simply are not enough, or simply not the point.

To return to Jane's story for a moment, we can see that even a woman as well educated and intelligent as Jane could allow herself to act as a received knower in relation to her feminist colleagues.

Since Jane herself found it "unthinkable" to betray another woman in the manner in which she finally was betrayed, she paid attention *only* to those messages she received that told her what she wanted to hear about her situation.

When Jane said she was "not sure" she really wanted to learn what her story could teach her, she meant that she did not want to give up her illusions about a magical family community.

"I finally realized that all along I believed that if I behaved well, so would everyone else," she admitted. "I had created some sort of magic umbrella. Now I realize that I might have been able to make alliances with other colleagues to reinforce me in case just what did happen should occur. But doing that then meant that I would have had to feel suspicious of the women I thought were my friends.

"Now," Jane continued, "I'm more aware that my own moral and ethical assumptions don't apply to everyone else. That would be nice, but realistically, I've had to give up expecting to be protected just because I'm behaving well.

However, knowing that has freed me, too. Now I feel proud of myself for acting ethically—I know I've made a choice, rather than acting out of fear."

Like Jane, many of us learn to gather information from external authorities. When we do so, we assume that *all* women do the same, that all women exist within a group of people who are told what to do, rather than people who do the telling. We assume that the loyalty practiced in such groups—loyalty created by oppression—functions within the larger context of the professional workplace.

However, although women, historically and currently, have been and are being discriminated against in the workplace, not all women suffer in the same way any longer. In fact, in order to enter the professional workplace at all, women need to give up their traditional identification as victims. They have to accept the real power and authority over people that is part and parcel of success at work.

As men have done, women are learning that professional friendship is distinctly different from personal friendship. While we should not assume that this distinction means becoming as ruthless as we believe men to be, it does mean we will have to be open to messages that interfere with our inherited self-definitions as good girls.

Ironically, the successful women who do not tell the stories about competitive losses have learned to communicate well. They are no longer received knowers. They no longer believe that what they feel is also what they think. They've learned to strike a balance between the outside voices telling them what to do and the inside voice telling them what to think about it.

In contrast, when we tell stories about competition with other women at work, we don't really seek to communicate at all. Instead, we seek reassurance and consolation. We seek to keep the world the way we feel most comfortable in it—trusting the authorities who tell us we are good girls, despite the fact that being good girls has earned us pain and disappointment. But the women who *don't* tell such stories have learned to hear even the messages that disturb their self-images. They are women who believe they are capable of forming their own opinions, who make reasoned evaluations using *all* available data; they are women who have learned that they can change as their circumstances change. They acknowledge their own competition.

They are women who compete to challenge themselves first, and because they must, last.

## COMPETITION AND ANXIETY

Women have been taught to face competition with each other with dread and anxiety.

Most would agree with Alexa, nineteen, who said, "I'll do anything to avoid competition with one of my friends, even drop out of a class if I feel there's no other way out." But even for Alexa, who studies at a small private college offering a variety of courses, dropping out is not really an acceptable way to handle the anxiety she feels competing with women.

At some point most of us, like Alexa, must face the world in which we live and work, where competition with both other women and men occurs in every public and private institution, from the family to the workplace.

Psychologists define anxiety as a feeling of helplessness and dependency in an overpowering, hostile world. We all know that when we feel anxious, our ability to express ourselves goes way down.

As Gabrielle, thirty, put it, "When I have to speak out in a meeting, my palms sweat and I turn bright red. Worst of all, my head becomes a jumble of noise. I can't remember what I wanted to say, and there's no way I can say anything that makes sense. I feel like I suddenly get stupid."

When women enter the workplace, anxiety becomes a fact of life. Not only are they stressed, just like men, about the quality of their work, but they are also anxious about relating to their colleagues.

As the stories told by women about competition reveal, when we compete with each other, our free-floating anxiety increases a thousandfold. At that level, communication becomes impossible; we're able to respond to each other only by "turning on" or "turning off," and shades of subtlety, or ambiguity, vanish from our repertoire of responses.

It's interesting to realize that such singularity also appears in the interactions between schizophrenic children and their parents. Although some recent research suggests a genetic or viral link to schizophrenia, the patterns of communication within schizophrenic families are marked by their inability to tolerate ambiguity. Parents in such families seem to deliver "double bind" messages to their children, in effect telling them, "You're damned if you do and damned if you don't." They're unable to tolerate playfulness from their children, and the consequence can be seen in the schizophrenic's perfectly literal perspective. To the schizophrenic mind, the world is either yes or no, black or white, up or down. There are no shades of gray.

This same intolerance of ambiguity appears in the stories women tell about competitive losses. There are no shades of gray here, either, although they do include sudden, baffling reversals. Friends suddenly become enemies; enemies become friends. No one is recognized as both. It becomes clear that neither betrayer nor betrayed is able to tolerate ambiguity. *Both* participated in setting up a win-or-lose situation, with no middle ground available for either. These stories describe the schizophrenia of the workplace, which women experience perhaps more acutely than men.

Trained to value trust, when women compete and lose, we respond to the same "double bind" messages received by schizophrenic children: we hear society tell us we should work hard and be good girls, even as we realize that being a good girl insures failure.

Now caught in a vicious circle, we further insure failure as our ability to communicate with ourselves and our colleagues rapidly deteriorates. At this level of anxiety, we become frightened. We believe we must succeed *here*, or we'll never succeed again. Our sense of multiple alternatives is drastically reduced. Unfortunately, the more anxious and frightened we become, the more we provoke resistance to our desires from the person with whom we are in competition, as well as from the workplace in general.

Both competitors, responding to the high levels of anxiety in the system, cease to care about each other. Instead, each cares only for herself. Thus, our competition can become genuinely ruthless, without mercy, and in disregard of justice or integrity. At that point, each of us fights for her own survival.

When one suffers from high anxiety, the other person's resistance seems to stiffen automatically, but when one is able to decrease the anxiety, one often discovers that resistance vanishes completely.

Women who've learned to compete successfully with other women have also learned not to depend on a single outcome from the competition. They are able to decrease their anxiety because they do not cling desperately to one imagined result. They go *with* the competition, not against it.

## MAKING YOUR BOUNDARIES CLEAR: COMPETING FOR DISTANCE AND DIRECTION

Family therapist Edwin H. Friedman believes that communication is an "emotional phenomenon." In addition to its being affected by anxiety, the capacity to communicate is linked, he feels, with direction and distance. By distance, Friedman means that when people are too far apart *or* too close together, communication decreases.

For example, mothers often can't understand why they have to repeat to their families, over and over, simple directions such as "Clean up your room," "Clear the table," or "Take out the garbage." Repetition doesn't work, as mothers know well to their weary despair. Their families literally are "mother deaf," because they are so close to the mother that they cannot hear what she says as a separate communication arriving at their ears from an independent outside source.

Women who work together often experience a similar "mother deafness" since their relationships are formed according to family models, with the same type of closeness.

Kim, for example, a top-notch hairdresser with many years of experience, reports that when she attempts to train younger female hairdressers, the younger women can't seem to understand her directions. "Even when I stand with them and move the comb in their hands, they can't understand what I'm trying to teach. I know they can't be that dumb," she said.

She's right. The women she trains are not "dumb."

They're competing with her by not learning the craft she teaches—not because they don't want to, but because they are too close to hear her. In Kim's hairdressing salon the distinction between senior women and their younger colleagues is not well marked. The younger women unconsciously become "mother deaf." When they fail to understand Kim's directions, they compete with her for her position. Tacitly, they assert they are her equal.

Yet we also can see that Kim and her young assistants, viewed more affirmatively, *use* their competition to attain distance. Their competition becomes a form of tension between them, defining boundaries they need, boundaries about which neither they nor their workplace is aware.

When we experience competition from our colleagues, most of us automatically assume the motivation to be malicious. However, the motivation might well be to get some breathing room. Kim's younger colleagues don't *all* want to take her job: instead, some want the space to learn it well enough to find a place of their own.

Working women who experience situations of too much distance suffer from another version of "mother deafness." Women who believe that working hard and doing what they're told insures success have distanced themselves out of earshot of the messages they need to hear about success in the workplace. All they can "hear," and therefore act upon, are their own assumptions. Often these are the women who become the "office martyr," like Mary Catharine, who was hired by a large university to teach a certain set of courses but took on an extra administrative task running a program indirectly related to her formal position.

Mary Catharine believed that she was pitching in, and she spent three years focused on administrative duties while she neglected her own writing and research. At the same time, Tamara, hired during the same month as Mary Catharine, concentrated on writing and publishing a book, refusing all optional administrative tasks that interfered with her writing time. In a competition for popularity, Mary Catharine was the hands-down winner. Her willingness to overburden herself made her enormously well liked among her colleagues, while Tamara, although well respected, was considered arrogant and overly ambitious.

But when both women finally came up for tenure, their competition was negotiated very differently. Mary Catharine discovered that although her colleagues appreciated her hard work, the tenure decision would be based on the scholarship she had failed to accomplish. She lost her position because she could not "hear" the assumptions made by her university. Instead, she "heard" the message that being a "good girl" was more important than her own ambitions. Attempting to serve her colleagues, she failed to serve herself. And she felt critically betrayed by her colleagues, particularly when Tamara was awarded tenure. Despite the definitions made about her, Tamara had realized that she needed to create a boundary between herself and her workplace that would promote her success.

As Kim's, Mary Catharine's, and Tamara's stories demonstrate, the right distance for effective communication is achieved by making one's own boundaries clear. When your boundaries are well defined, you know what you want, and what you are willing to do to get it. You know both what the people who surround you want, and what they want *from* you. When your boundaries are clear, you neither try to define someone else's boundaries, nor do you allow them to define yours.

When women tell stories about competitive losses we often sound desperate. We are tied to the competition that devastated us because, unconsciously, we insist on remaining too close to it to understand thoroughly how our own failure to establish boundaries assisted our betrayal.

Instead, we often try to reconstruct the same situation again, and this time we work harder, endure more, and pay even more attention to what other people ask us to do. In effect, we wind up competing harder in exactly the same way that caused so much trouble in the first place. But competing harder doesn't work. In order to compete more effectively, we must increase the information we take in and give out. We must define our jobs both in our own terms and in relation to workplace demands.

Defining our boundaries also affects the direction of communication. Dr. Friedman writes that direction in communication explains why, when we give very good advice to other people, they so often ignore us.

For example, your best friend is about to get married. You gather your courage together, and tell her that her fiancé is not the man she believes him to be. He's impulsive—she thinks he's exciting. He's stingy—she thinks he's careful. He's mean—she thinks he's strong.

Worse yet, ten years later, their divorce proves you were absolutely right. As an outside observer, you were able to see what she could not. But your communication did not get through. Your friend was moving, at the speed of light, away from your message as she moved with equal alacrity toward her lover. She could hear only his voice.

\*     \*     \*

At work the woman who loses the competition pursues the woman who wins in the same way you pursued your friend with your well-founded, completely correct, and totally dismissed advice.

The dominant theme of the stories women tell about their competitive losses—"I was betrayed"—proves that they try to speak, as they tried to work, in only *one* direction. When communication occurs in one direction, it fails. When competition occurs in one direction, *you* fail.

Trying to explain their loss, women reveal that at work, their effort to communicate with colleagues or supervisors always went in the same direction, toward convincing the other woman about the value of their work, or the virtue of their position. Because they were locked into a single direction, they lost the flexibility necessary to make communication—and competition—effective.

Fundamentally, the women who tell stories about competitive losses talk about a world that's "not fair." The only direction they travel in is "not fair." But women who succeed in the workplace are able to switch directions, because they've changed their perspective on the workplace. The professional workplace is indeed "not fair" to most women working within it, but successful women see it in terms of utility. Fairness may be an issue, but fairness is not the only point.

## COMPETITIVE RESILIENCE

Ironically, when fairness becomes one among several issues for working women, genuine justice and loyalty are possible. Research has demonstrated that the capacity to care for younger members of a species and the capacity for playfulness develop during the same stage of evolution in mammals. Playfulness, therefore, is significantly connected to intimate bonding and caring behavior.

We feel intimate with another person with whom we can joke and be "silly." We are willing to care for that person. We are willing to give him or her our loyalty. We want to treat the person justly.

Emotionally, playfulness is based on being resilient in our responses. When we are playful we are able to change direction quickly and easily. We can move from serious conversation to joking and back again. But when women compete with each other, we often lose the resilience of our responses. We become deadly serious. None of the women who tell stories about competitive losses sees any humor in her situation.

Of course, it's difficult to laugh at losing money, job, and reputation. Nevertheless, without the ability to understand anything about our situations as funny at all, we have no way to recuperate, no way to learn how to do it differently next time.

Women who compete successfully have learned that competition is the game played in the workplace. At some level, games are supposed to be fun.

"I think of it as being on a roller coaster," said Janet, forty-eight, head of the very successful advertising agency she started ten years ago. "Sometimes I'm up, sometimes I'm down, but I always enjoy playing. In fact, occasionally, excluding the financial problems, it can be as much fun to lose as to win. Figuring out where I went wrong can be really funny. Often I can't believe I missed a simple move. I suppose that I don't really question my competence, so understanding a stupid move doesn't threaten me. It spurs me on and provides a challenge."

Although Janet thinks her resilience is based on her competence, without resilience she would not be competent. When Janet laughs at herself, she laughs at her realization that a particular failure had as much to do with being stuck in one response as with a difficult client. Often, when we find ourselves in competition with other women, we activate a section of the brain that denies playfulness and resiliency. We act out of the primitive limbic system, which developed prior to mammalian evolution. In other words, when we compete with other women we think reactively. We lose the capacity to change direction, to use our imaginations, or to change our perspectives. In contrast, the successful women who retain resilience and playfulness in competitive situations at work move beyond assuming that all information is derived from an outside authority. They are, as Belenky et al. call them in *Women's Ways of Knowing* (page 87), "procedural knowers." They accumulate knowledge by focusing on procedures, skills, and techniques.

Procedural knowers ask how many different ways they can formulate a question, how many different perspectives they can use to resolve an issue. Unlike received knowers, procedural knowers "are interested not just in *what* people think, but in *how* people go about forming their ideas and opinions."

The women who tell the stories about competitive losses believe that they pay attention to outside authority. Procedural knowers go farther. They integrate external information with their own ideas and desires. Their ability to compete is enhanced because they rely on self *and* other, and because they can change direction *between* self and other.

Ironically, when we move into this stage, we become

better competitors because we strengthen our capacity for empathy.

Although we usually feel that competition disrupts our ability to empathize with each other, we're wrong. Empathy depends on knowing what one wants oneself before one can be resilient enough to know what the other person wants. When we rely on outside authorities to tell us what to do, our capacity for empathy, as well as communication and competition, is strikingly impaired. Relying on outside authority means understanding only what other people want *from* you.

Women who rely on outside authorities lose the playfulness derived from appreciating the gap between the way we see ourself and the way we are seen by others. When we are unable to laugh at ourselves, we lose both our empathic ability and our imaginations.

It is not competition, necessarily, that disrupts empathy. Instead, it's the failure to understand that another woman is competing with us, to understand that we, too, are competing.

When we base our behavior on knowledge about what the other person wants, as well as on knowledge about what the other person wants *from* us, we can choose whether or not we want to enter a competition. We can choose how we will conduct ourselves if we join it.

When we insist on telling the stories about our competitive losses, in effect, we reveal that we cannot stand to compete, but somehow, the women who are *not* talking have learned to lower their anxiety when they face competition. When they do so, they effectively increase their ability to communicate, both with themselves and with other women.

In fact, it is precisely because they are able to imagine actively a variety of alternatives possible in any given situation, *including the possibility of failure*, that their competition is so often successful.

The stories told by workplace Cinderellas are horrifying not only because they focus on betrayal and treachery, disaster and loss, but because they are closed—they make the listener want to leave the world they describe. They make a female listener vow never to trust another woman again. They are inflexible, anxious, and single-minded stories because the teller is always and can only be a victim in their telling.

The real aim of these stories is to make the other woman take responsibility for the disaster. But like most efforts to make other people responsible for what they resist, this one also fails. From the outset, it is doomed exactly because the effort preempts the responsibility.

As mothers discover when they nag their children to do household chores, the nagging makes Mother responsible for the task. In the same way, when we become obsessed about our competitive losses, we take responsibility *away* from the women we believe betrayed us. We make it our issue. And when we are obsessed and desperate, we compete in the same way we tell our stories. We leave our own boundaries unclear in an attempt to shift responsibility for the competition onto the other woman. Inevitably, it is the woman who shifts responsibility who shoulders the burden. Like many of the women who told their stories in this chapter, it is the woman locked into her own perspective, too close to her own emotions and too far from the expectations governing the workplace, who bears the brunt of competition among and between women—who loses job, money, reputation, and happiness.

It is important to recognize here that the women who win competitions with other women because they have fully accepted and fully exploit patriarchal marketplace ethics *also* lose, both in larger and smaller ways. Although they may gain money and career advancement, they lose themselves.

These are the women who feel most fraudulent because, in fact, they are. They've become what they believe men want them to be at work—other men. They've given up the female virtues of nurturance, compassion, and empathy for what amounts to a mess of pottage.

Douglas LaBier, in his study of mental and emotional health in the corporate workplace, found that hugely successful women could be even more emotionally disturbed than hugely successful men. Although the men in LaBier's study became authoritarian and sadistic, they affirmed a distortion of masculine identity in the process of their success. The women, in contrast, affirmed nothing beyond a perverted set of values, becoming more and more empty inside.

Although women want success in the professional workplace, they do not want to become caricatures of successful men. If competition with each other is a necessary component of professional success, women will have to make it a *female* competition, employing female talents and satisfying female needs for connection despite the encouragement we receive to separate.

## CREATIVE COMPETITION IN THE WORKPLACE

In a recent survey of the most powerful women in Washington, D.C., conducted by the *Washingtonian Magazine*, more than eighty of the one hundred women studied reported that they had experienced either gender or race discrimination, or both, in the workplace. But only six of those women sought out their organization's internal complaint process for remedy. *None* filed a legal action.

Although legal remedies have been critically instrumental in improving working conditions for women, these successful women revealed that they refused to become "stuck" in their grievances. Instead, they found another way out.

They learned new technical languages. They assessed their skills and put these to use in unexpected ways, as Kate Michelman, head of the National Abortion Rights Action League, did, who reported that she "merely built on the organizational and communications skills she had developed earlier."

These successful women, like Ann Jones, now a partner in a major law firm specializing in communications law, extended their expertise into new branches of a familiar field. "I'm probably only happy when I'm in over my head," she said. "I've done it to myself so many times."

The *Washingtonian* survey revealed that successful women "often attribute their success to the chances they took—their willingness to change direction from the standard career plan."

Also, these successful women did not mention competing with other women. Instead, they talked about their mentors. They focused on cooperation, not competition, although there can be no doubt that in their careers, these very successful women experienced competition with and from other women. However, competition did not cripple them.

They would agree with Lauren, forty-nine, whose successful tax law practice serves some of the largest nonprofit organizations in Washington, D.C. "I keep my sense of being threatened to myself," Lauren said. "Gossip undermines the confidence I have in the person telling it to me. It makes me feel that she would say the same things about me if she had the chance. And I assume that other women would respond in the same way if I was the gossiper."

Like Lauren, most successful women are careful about competition in the workplace. They do not deny that competition exists, or that they, as well as other women, practice it.

In competitive situations, though, these women are creative. They know that really dangerous situations arise when competition is *unconscious*, and when their own success depends on some other woman's defeat. They work to create situations in which everyone thrives.

Competition in the workplace can be considered an art.

For women, it falls into the category of all those things that, since one *must* do them, should be done well, perhaps even with grace, elegance, and charity.

The power of art lies in its ability to stimulate the imagination. The great writer makes her reader work to bring the book alive. The great painter carefully provokes her viewer to make the painting cohere. Great art emphasizes the unsaid—it asks, rather than answers, questions. It communicates through ambiguity. It engenders multiple interpretations.

When we learn to practice competition as an art, we stop protecting ourselves from it. It ceases to feel quite so dangerous. It ceases to make us feel desperate and out of control. We become better negotiators because we learn to distinguish the difference between our needs and our negotiating positions.

Practicing competition as an art can make it creative. Right now, when we compete, we concentrate on receiving answers to questions like "Am I doing a good job?" "Am I a good girl?" "Do you like me?" We believe that winning or losing is determined by the result of the competition, that success is determined by the bottom line.

This is a rigidity that acts directly against our socialization. When we focus on getting answers rather than asking questions, we focus on disconnection.

Women don't enjoy watching the bottom line. Instead, we get real satisfaction from paying attention to the process. Ignoring the process—the relationship between the two people competing—in favor of the competitive outcome denies us access to female creativity. We are talented at making relationships work. We are creative in putting people together and keeping them that way.

When we concentrate on the bottom line in a competition, we work against our real strengths and restrict our creative potential to doing what we do not do well.

Instead of focusing on bottom-line results, Mary Ann, forty-seven, a successful management consultant, concentrates on outcomes like "continuing education, self-development, and creative challenge." But this sort of concentration is new for Mary Ann. While shifting her attention away from the bottom line has enhanced her creativity at work, she reports that she has learned to do so only after nearly two decades of struggle at work.

"I was always on the edge of desperation at work," Mary Ann said. "Every decision felt dire, every move I made brought with it an anguished self-examination.

"Gradually I learned to distinguish between what I really wanted and what my job told me I wanted. A lot of this, of course, was possible because I started making enough money so that I wasn't panicked all the time.

"But as I relaxed, I realized that all competitions didn't affect me in the same way. For instance, when I lost a client to another woman, I really suffered. But when I lost the client to a man, it was much easier. Gradually I realized that in any situation where I had to compete with another woman, I would panic, and probably lose.

"Now, because I'm so aware of the way competition with another woman makes me feel, I use the feelings as a signal that I have to calm down. What's really interesting is that once I'm calm, I can focus on what really counts for me, instead of desperately trying to win just so that my opponent won't.

"Now I'm actually much more successful financially than I used to be. But what's really important is that I enjoy working a whole lot more."

Mary Ann's creativity at work was enhanced because she learned that her competitiveness was not global. Like most women, when Mary Ann found herself in a competitive situation, she found her anxiety so high that she mistook her response to a particular situation for a general response. Instead, learning to distinguish those situations that raised her anxiety allowed her to separate them from situations that did not produce panic. In turn, knowing that there were times when she was not panicked made it possible for her to examine the situations producing the most anxiety and see that, in her case, it was competition with another woman that made her act in ways out of her own control. Noticing this allowed her to reflect *before* acting out her feelings of desperation and panic. By discovering self-control, Mary Ann discovered self-empowerment.

* * *

When we feel empowered, we are able to use our creativity actively to enhance and change our environment. We no longer feel that adaptation to a situation that is making us unhappy is the only possible solution. And women who feel empowered are far more interested in obtaining the sort of power that makes things happen and far less interested in the sort of power that controls other people.

For women, creativity is related directly to communication. When women communicate effectively, they have a sense of working with, rather than against, the world around them.

"I always have an opinion," said Nancy, forty-six, whose executive position with a large government institution that funds grants brings her into contact with dozens of people each week. "I realize that other people may disagree with me, but I know that they will be able to hear what I say. After twenty-odd years working in large institutions, I think the most valuable skill I've learned is how to talk to other people."

Communicating with other people means finding an appropriate distance from which to speak, neither too close to the other to assume that the other person thinks exactly as you do, nor too far to hear that she may not.

It means being able to tolerate ambiguity, and to be flexible both in sending and receiving messages.

It means decreasing the free-floating anxiety in the workplace by decreasing your own anxiety.

It means paying attention to internal messages locating anxiety as a response to *particular* situations, rather than allowing yourself to be overwhelmed.

It means determining what *you* want rather than accepting that workplace demands necessarily match your own.

Communication—and competition—is most creative

when it is not desperate. The women who communicate best know that they win some and they lose some—the point really *is* how the game is played.

## CHANGING COMPETITIVE BEHAVIOR: EVERY WOMAN COUNTS

Change in social behavior *is* possible. It occurs when a critical mass is achieved, when more of us are made unhappy than are made happy by current conditions.

However, the notion of critical mass is a sociological abstraction. When change really happens in our own lives, it happens because we have decided, at last, to do something about our lives. We have decided that we will not tolerate, not for one second longer, living in ways that make us extremely unhappy.

Yet what seem like our own independent decisions depend on support: we can change our own lives only when we are supported by our environment. We can change our own lives when we can identify ourselves as part of a larger group of very unhappy people. For many, many working women—a critical mass—change is happening because the demands of their working lives conflict directly with demands of their personal lives.

Particularly because of the conflict between raising children and professional advancement, many working women feel they can no longer endure their lives of enormous stress and pressure.

Right now, enough women—a whole generation—are seriously burdened by this conflict. Because the problem is so widespread, every woman can make a difference.

"Most of us will pitch in when someone has a real problem," said Cheryl, thirty-two. "When I pick up my son at nursery school, I'm ready to bring home with us one of his little friends whose mother had to stay on at her office, or whose baby-sitter didn't show up. But other mothers seem to get even more anxious when they're stressed like that. I've had the most insane conversations with other mothers about car pools, where some of them try to figure out driving time down to five-minute differentials."

Cheryl is not describing women who wish to harm each other, or who gain when another woman loses. Instead she describes women burdened to the point of breakdown by the pressures of scheduling family and professional life, as well as the overwhelming guilt such scheduling often produces. When women are overstressed by family responsibilities, they turn against each other, just as they do when they are overanxious at work. Yet, in the same way it happens at work, when women mistake their anxiety for competition, the person they harm most is themselves.

Right now, in the midst of what the sociologist Arlie Hochschild calls a "stalled revolution," the people who can best help women with the problem of child rearing and professional obligations are other women.

The workplace can become more humane. There are solutions to the problem. They include flexible work schedules, job sharing, and on-site child-care centers. More immediately, humanizing the workplace means reviving the notion of sisterhood, making it workable rather than an unattainable ideal.

Professional sisters recognize that they compete with each other. Professional sisters perceive the workplace as a place where women are at a disadvantage, and therefore they realize that women need to support each other. Professional sisters recognize that support means empathizing with the real conditions of women's lives, rather than assuming that support means only *receiving* assistance.

Right now, humanizing the workplace falls to women most affected by the contrast between traditional ideals about child rearing and professional obligations. These are the women on the barricades of change because their *real* lives are those lived with the most difficulty.

These women report that they depend on the support, sympathy, and understanding that come more frequently from female than from male supervisors and colleagues.

"My boss is very supportive," said Nedra, forty-three, a Washington lobbyist. "She makes sure that I get projects I can complete during my three-day work week, because she knows that I need to be home with my kids on the other two days. She also makes sure that the information flow in the office works very well, so when I come in I know I'll have all the data I missed when I was out. She realizes that kind of support is invaluable for both of us—I do a good job and she has a good staff."

The kind of support Nedra describes indicates that our society is changing, that our notions of who should work, when, and for how long, are becoming elements in a new system of values about work and family life.

Change in large social structures occurs when a part of the overall structure ceases to function as an agent for stabilization and instead becomes the fulcrum for change.

As Cheryl's and Nedra's comments reveal, competition between women at work and because of work now exists precisely at that juncture between status quo and change. When women compete with each other at work, they compete with precisely the person whom they need in order to make their working lives possible.

According to Erich Fromm, writing in *Beyond the Chains of Illusion*, every society develops a system of categories that determine the issues of which people within it will allow themselves to become aware. This system operates "like a socially conditioned filter: experience cannot enter awareness unless it can penetrate this filter." In other words, what we allow ourselves to know must fit into a social category already in existence, but competition between women in the workplace does not fit in.

We can understand when women compete with each other for men, for attractiveness, about their clothes or their bodies, when they compete in private, indirectly and covertly.

Competition between women that is private, personal, and covert fits into the social category defining femininity. Feminine women are not public beings. Femininity means personal responsiveness, and feminine wiles imply manipulation.

However, we *cannot* understand when women compete *out in the open* with each other. It is an entirely new phenomenon.

In fact, we don't even have the words to describe the emotions women experience when they compete with each other in public arenas like the workplace.

In general, as Fromm writes in *Beyond the Chains of Illusion*, "our language just does not give us words which we need to describe many visceral [gut-level] experiences which do not fit our scheme of thoughts."

When women compete with each other at work we feel it

in our guts. And this is a good thing for us. Feeling our competition viscerally means that we are *unable* to make it impersonal; therefore, public competition between us remains distinctly different from public competition between men.

Despite all the books and experts advising us to separate our personal feelings from our professional competitions, women remain responsive to and responsible for our competitions *because* we remain personally involved with our competitors. However, we possess no adequate translation of our gut feelings. Instead, we are forced to reduce our complicated emotions to statements about betrayal and treachery. We are forced to deny our own competitiveness, because admitting it interferes with our inherited categories.

When we are not able to express our emotions, we are distanced from our own feelings. Because we have no language for them, certain feelings are not permitted to reach consciousness, but instead are filtered out long before we need to speak about them.

Nevertheless, although we may not have the words to talk about our feelings, they're still there, but we don't permit ourselves to acknowledge them. Instead, we develop physical symptoms, like ulcers and heart attacks, migraine headaches and back pains. We sleep badly and eat too much or too little. And when we allow ourselves to repress a conflict from conscious awareness, we are guided by our fear of isolation and ostracism from our group.

As a species, human beings are so terrified of isolation that we will literally shut off conscious awareness of individual reality in order to be part of the group.

When women compete at work, we are in the process of forming a new social "group." When new groups form, disrupting old relationships, emotional pain can feel over-whelming.

When women compete with each other at work, we experience a situation of enormous emotional and psychic conflict.

On the one hand, most of us deeply desire to conform to traditional standards of feminine behavior. We deeply believe that women don't compete with each other out in the open, and that those women who do are humiliated and abandoned.

On the other hand, women who fail to compete in the workplace suffer the same fate. We are isolated by defeat and ostracized by failure.

Repressing conscious awareness of our competition no longer works. It no longer delivers security, nor does it keep anxiety and fear unconscious.

Telling women not to take their competition personally doesn't work, either. Women *need* to feel their competition personally. Since connection with other people is a funda-mental part of female identity, women are unable to sepa-rate relationships into the impersonal and the personal. When women make their relationships impersonal, they lose themselves. Instead, we need to understand that our workplace competition, out in the open and personally felt, is the dynamic for real change in our society, both for us and for the workplace in general.

When we compete with each other at work, our compe-tition places us precisely at the location where human values conflict with social "necessities."

As more and more women attain positions of authority, it is likely that they will experience less and less insecurity when they think of themselves as working women. In addition, given the increasing numbers of working women with young children, it is likely that the "stalled revolution" will move a notch forward. Women will insist not only on equal pay for equal work, but also on equal responsibility for child care and household work.

When they do, it is possible that the combined voices of men and women will be heard in the workplace, insisting that raising the next generation is a responsibility our society shares with individual families.

Doris Lessing notes in *Prisons We Choose to Live Inside* (page 73), "It is individuals who change societies, give birth to ideas, who, standing out against the tides of opinion, change them."

Every woman counts in this struggle. Standing in the midst of what feel like impenetrable social systems wrenching her emotions and her life, every woman can decide to make her life different.

Every woman can decide that the competition that makes her "sick" can change. She can change it. She can understand that her very existence is a new social category, and that competing openly *with* personal responsibility can make the workplace humane.

Large social changes usually happen in small, almost invisible ways. Barbara, thirty-nine, who works as an administrative assistant, offers an example of what looks like one woman's change, which, in fact, reflects a society in transition.

"I've had twelve female bosses in the last eighteen years," Barbara said. "I guess eleven out of the twelve were negative. Most of them seemed to operate on the 'queen bee' syndrome. They had achieved a position of power, but they were so insecure that they acted like they could be the only powerful woman around. The rest of us were drones. "But my boss now is different. Unlike some of the others, Margo doesn't flirt with the men at the top, and she doesn't turn into a little girl when she needs something from them. She's consistently encouraging to me; she cares without being cloying about it. She makes critical comments with humor and makes sure that she doesn't humiliate or embarrass her staff. She lets me know that she considers a bad piece of work a stage, not a fixed state.

"Maybe most important of all, Margo doesn't try to hide her own insecurities. She doesn't punish us for all the hardships she endured on the way up. She never scapegoats her staff. When she manages us, she compares her insecurities with ours—she gets us to do good work because she admits that her authority and her humanity are integrated."

Barbara laughed after describing her boss. "I kept waiting for the other shoe to drop. You know, after the probation period, when you're really tied in, that's when most bosses show their real power to their employees. But Margo never wavers from being Margo. Even when she has to deal with her own boss, who's a very difficult woman, she's simple, direct, and without pretense. And she'll apologize when she gets irritable. She lets us know that she can be as stressed as we are, but that it's not our fault."

As a supervisor, Margo demonstrates the difference one woman can make in the workplace. Rather than denying that she competes with her employees, she keeps her competition *personal*—she implicates herself in the competition. She understands that the competition her authority creates is her personal responsibility. She makes the rules

that make good working conditions—and good work—
possible in her office. She creates a relationship system that
permits all the women working with her to thrive.

### THE EMPEROR'S NEW CLOTHES: CHANGING COMPETITION INSTEAD OF CHANGING YOURSELF

Listening to Barbara describe her boss, we understand that
women can improve working conditions both for themselves and for other women. This is an optimism reflected in
the ideas about self and work possessed by very young
women in our society, those between eighteen and twenty-
nine.

According to an extensive survey conducted by the *New
York Times* and reported on in the issues of August 21 and
22, 1989, these younger women are "at least as likely as
men to call their work a career.... Only half of them
agreed that 'men still run almost everything and usually
don't include women when important decisions are
made,' " a view held by solid majorities of older women in
the survey. And about a quarter of the younger women, far
more than in the older group, said, "Nothing is slighted
when a woman combines work, marriage, and children."

Of course, as any "older" woman would be quick to
point out, the majority of these younger women have not
experienced combining children, marriage, and career.
However, what the younger women articulate is a real
spirit of hope about the existence of women in the workplace. They believe they are here to stay.

They also express a genuine optimism about remaining
*women* at work. These younger women are not hoping
simply to have an easier time than their mothers. Nor are
they simply unappreciative of the struggle marking their

mothers' lives, a struggle that made their own working identities possible. Nor are they naive. Instead, they are making an appraisal of social conditions from a genuinely new perspective.

In contrast to women of their mothers' generation, many of these young women experienced a real balance of academic work, emotional relationships, and athletic activities. They have learned, as a fundamental part of their development, how to combine work and play, and how to play *seriously* with and against each other.

While they have yet to encounter, in large numbers, the stresses and difficulties of work and child rearing, they arrive at the workplace with a sense of female community different from that of their mothers. They arrive knowing that they can compete against each other and remain friends. They recognize the difference between the sort of competition that destroys other women and the competition supporting self while *challenging* another woman.

Experienced working women assume that the "realities" of working life will disabuse these younger women of their "ideals," but they forget the lesson contained in the old story about the emperor's new clothes. Only a *child* could see the reality of the emperor's nakedness because, since he was a child, he was new to the system.

Like the little boy in the story, these young women are saying that "reality" may not be real, that because things always have been done in a certain way doesn't mean that change is impossible, and they are willing to engage the reality of the workplace to make it more as they want it to be. Moreover, these young women will not be alone. They will be joined by their "older sisters" and by their "mothers."

Both the overwhelming burdens of combining family life

with professional careers and the ruthless "eat or be eaten" ethics of the workplace are causing a breakdown in women's lives fast becoming intolerable. Solutions that once seemed idealistic can become the bread of survival, given large enough numbers and someone to say out loud that the emperor is naked.

The youngest women in the workplace represent real change. It is possible that their different notions of women competing with each other will change rather than be changed by the workplace, that they will teach us that competition among women at work is a responsibility that *all* women must bear. Further, it is possible that when women recognize and admit their competition with each other, they will devise a way to practice it like women, not men—combining an ethic of success with an ethic of caring.

Understanding competition between women as a critical tool to change the workplace reflects an idea stated by Carol Gilligan, Jean Baker Miller, Dorothy Dinnerstein, and many other sociologists and psychologists who are studying female development. They have learned that in our society women do the emotional work, both for themselves and for the other people in their lives.

Women have known for a long time that they are responsible for feeling, while men are responsible for doing, but they haven't recognized the power to change social conditions their ability to feel, to experience emotion directly, gives them.

For example, Abby, thirty-seven, sold commercial real estate for a large company. All the other people working in her office were men. She believed, she said, that in order to succeed she had to straddle a fine line. She had to be as tough as her male colleagues, but also extremely feminine so she wouldn't threaten them in a way that would make them punish her.

Therefore, Abby was careful about her makeup and clothing at work. Her business suits conveyed a carefully mixed message, paraphrased as "I'm serious about my work, but not too serious to look pretty."

But the fine line Abby straddled didn't define her *feelings* about her work. When she found herself in competition for a piece of property with her colleagues, she was riven with an emotional distress they did not seem to feel at all.

As Abby remarks, "Even the men I considered my *friends* didn't care. The last time I lost out to a man, he was a good friend. And he certainly didn't need the business, while he knew that it meant a large part of my income for the whole year. He didn't even apologize for grabbing my client. He said my feelings were my problem."

Abby's colleague depended on her to do the feeling in their competition. He was able to display what most women would consider real disloyalty, apparently without a second thought. In contrast, Abby "felt" both her own loss *and* his lack of ethics. She was as upset that "he could do that to her" as she was about her financial loss. She discovered that in terms of her job, being "serious" about her work meant being without feelings—that the fine line she straddled between femininity and tough professionalism did not exist. She decided that the choice she had to make, between her feelings and her success, was unacceptable. She left that firm to join a smaller company staffed by women and men.

However, when enough "Abbys" become part of the large firm, they won't leave. Making personal decisions to feel *and* to succeed, they will change the assumptions governing workplace behavior.

Because women have direct access to their feelings, they are unable to fool themselves into thinking that a competition for power or self-aggrandizement does not harm another woman, another man—or themselves.

Right now, working women, forced to compete out in the open, also are forced to live with feelings of selfishness, disloyalty, and rampant egotism. They are forced to identify themselves, emotionally, as "bad" people, yet it is exactly those feelings that produce change.

Wanting to succeed and wanting to connect with other people is the conflict brought into sharp focus for working women.

Right now, as demonstrated by the youngest women in the *New York Times* survey, women are trying to solve this dilemma by changing *external* conditions rather than resorting to the time-honored feminine strategy of changing oneself to fit the environment.

Working women are no longer willing to live with feeling bad about themselves. This time, they are trying to improve the world even as they improve themselves.

## WORKING WOMEN WHO DON'T COMPETE WITH EACH OTHER

One of the most startling pieces of information I learned while researching for this book is that women don't compete with each other.

*Every* woman I interviewed firmly believed that *she* didn't compete with other women. Every woman changed her mind during our conversation.

Nevertheless, while it became obvious that we all compete with each other, I also recognized that some of the women whom I interviewed practiced their competition in a way that made it secondary. Their competition did not define their working lives.

"I work because without work I wouldn't exist," said Cassie, fifty-one, an attorney whose practice focuses on public advocacy for the homeless.

"I love my work. I feel somehow it keeps me in touch with the real world," said Irene, forty-four, who teaches remedial reading to students in a large inner-city high school.

"I guess work gives me self-esteem," said Hope, forty-six, a lawyer representing nonprofit organizations.

"Work is so wonderful because when I'm in the classroom, I forget everything else. All my worries drop away, at least during class period," said Darcy, forty-three, a university professor.

Cassie, Irene, Hope, and Darcy are all working women. Two of them, Cassie and Hope, began to prepare for their careers when they were children.

Both grew up in relatively privileged households in which their education and development was supported and encouraged. Both were able to identify, in particular, with fathers who were successful and powerful men in their own professions, who encouraged their daughters to make their way in the wider world beyond marriage and family.

In contrast, Irene and Darcy realized their professional aspirations much later in their lives. Both returned to school for graduate training after a long struggle to separate their feelings of public incompetence from their real talents and abilities. While they, like Cassie and Hope, grew up in families materially comfortable enough to support their educations, both were discouraged from identifying themselves as women who work.

Nevertheless, Cassie spoke for all four women when she insisted, "Work is my salvation." Cassie means that work provides her with a steady sense of existence. When she is working, she knows that her words have weight and her actions have consequence.

For Cassie, Hope, Irene, and Darcy, work is not bound to the achievements of other women. Instead, it is precisely their work that gives them the self-esteem they need to make their relationships with other women, both friends and colleagues, crucially important to them.

For a period of two years, Irene and Darcy shared an office in Darcy's university, where Irene worked "on loan" from her school as an education consultant. "Knowing that I would go in every morning and talk to Darcy was a big part of the job," said Irene. "Although we weren't in direct competition, we did share many of the same students, so there might have been a competition for popularity. But we realized very quickly that because we were both very skilled, we could use each other to enhance our students' experience at school. I generally directed my students into Darcy's classes, and she had me come into her classes, so I could give her feedback on her teaching, several times."

Darcy agreed. "I *did* feel some initial resentment toward Irene. Before she came, I felt like I was the most popular teacher in the department. But having her around was a challenge. Competing with her in a way that would make her less effective would have hurt me. Knowing she was so good made me do even better."

Although Cassie and Hope, both lawyers, have never worked in the same office, they too experienced overlap in their careers. "When I first started working, I joined a large corporate firm," said Hope. "Cassie was a neighbor. She advised me to leave the firm because the work would be degrading. I did go through a period when just seeing Cassie made me feel competitive, because I was struggling with my own doubts about my firm, and I wanted to prove she was wrong. When I was able, finally, to separate my own desires from having to compete with Cassie, I understood that she had been right all along."

Like Irene and Darcy, Hope and Cassie learned that their relationship was far more important than their competition, and it meant that each woman was able to alter her relationships with other women at work.

I believed these women when they said they did not compete with other women at work because they meant that their competition with other women was not nearly as important as their own work. They knew the difference between when they worked because they loved it, and when they worked to compete.

They were able to decide—consciously, rationally, and reflectively—what they wanted to do when they were in competition. They were able to use their competitiveness to challenge and be challenged by the other women with whom they worked.

It was not simple coincidence that led Cassie, Hope, Irene, and Darcy into the kind of work that helps other people even as it helps themselves.

"When I was in that large corporate firm," said Hope, "I didn't feel a sense of purpose. It was somehow not significant just to work for a paycheck. I wanted a different sort of power."

"I want to change the world," said Cassie. "I realize that sounds grandiose, and God knows that even after twenty years of fighting to get poor people into decent housing, I still see precious little real social change. But when I win a case, I feel fantastic. I've made a difference. Even when

I lose I know I've pushed the discourse a little further ahead."

Irene and Darcy agreed. "When a class goes well, I know that I've really affected my students, perhaps for the rest of their lives. I often meet former students who tell me how much my classes meant to them. That's what work is all about for me," said Darcy.

Cassie, Hope, Irene, and Darcy learned that work delivers power, but for them, power is connected intricately with empowering other people, so they chose to practice their professions in a way that combines power for themselves with power for others. "That defines work for me," added Irene.

Although working in a "helping profession" does not automatically mean that women are "better" people, it does help us understand that defining work as a way to empower self and other can diminish the sort of cutthroat competition women fear from themselves and each other. As Carol Gilligan writes, when women realize that power for the self *must* precede empowering others, they move to a new stage of maturity: they realize the difference between being "of service" and being subservient.

Being of service means valuing oneself. It means valuing one's competence and achievements in such a way that another woman's achievements are no longer felt as threatening. It means not feeling diminished by another woman's talents.

Starting with a sense of success rather than a sense of failure creates an understanding that competition with other women is a necessity, but not necessarily an evil, because *you* make that choice.

Being of service means reconceiving the economic system we live within as a system of plenty, instead of a system of scarcity.

Cassie, Hope, Irene, and Darcy all demonstrated their belief that they thrived when the women working with them also succeeded. Because they imagined that the system *could* offer something to each of them, in their working lives they made sure it did so. Even women working in the same office, working in situations designed to provoke desperate competition between them, can make that choice.

For example, the publishing industry is both notoriously competitive and sexist. Even today, the lower echelons of most publishing houses are staffed predominantly by women. For most women working in publishing, the way up is through another woman's job. Also, the pie is very limited. In this industry, a woman's job usually still defines the limits of a woman's rise. But Lena, thirty-eight, a senior editor at a major publishing house, believes, "Without Paula [Lena's assistant], I couldn't do my job."

Making that statement, Lena demonstrates the change women can bring to the workplace. If Lena were a woman defined by competition, she might feel that Paula wanted to learn as much as she could in order to take Lena's job. Instead, Lena says, "Having Paula around makes it possible for me to do very good work. There's enough room for both of us—I intend to make sure of that."

# Chapter
# 5

# Sisters and Friends

"Left to ourselves ... we hanker for friends."
—*Lewis Thomas*

## THE DREAM OF SISTERHOOD

Alice, Frances, and I are having dinner. Our dinners are very special to us. Dinner is an excuse. Mostly, we eat bread and the salad we put together out of odds and ends from each refrigerator.

We plan to be there, though. We know we are a group, although we have never, nor would we ever, identify ourselves as such. Several years ago we tried to name ourselves, but it didn't work out. Somehow, we are uneasy thinking of ourselves as a group: too much structure and too much explicit exclusion of other women.

Too much including ourselves. We don't exactly want to know what makes us so special to each other. We are pleased that each of us has other close and intimate female friends, who sometimes overlap among us, who sometimes come to dinner.

We like to think that natural affinity draws us, quite naturally, together. We like to feel that the comfort, support, and affirmation we offer each other is spontaneous, that we do not premeditate our friendship.

Really, we know better.

Each of us is an active friend. Now, when we all are in our forties and fifties, we know we choose each other. We know we continue to choose every time we set aside time from our work and our families to pay attention to each other.

We are present at the big events—weddings, graduations, funerals—and at the small events—a bad day, a minor professional success, conflict with ex-spouses, children, and husbands. We know we are important witnesses for each other.

We feel like sisters—sort of. We feel the way we imagine sisters ought to feel about each other.

This chapter is about sisters *and* friends, rather than one or the other, because I have come to believe that women choose our friends to correct the relationships we experienced with our "real" sisters. Even when we don't have sisters of our own, we long for sisterhood.

For most women, sisters and friends are intricately connected. It was not simple accident that led the feminist movement to call the bond between women "sisterhood," yet the notion of feminist sisterhood often leaves us with an aching sense of distress. It denies what women know: that we can be spiteful, mean, and malicious. We know that calling ourselves "sisters" often does not interfere with behavior toward other women that shames us.

When we think of each other as sisters, we dwell in the dream of sisterhood. We deny real life with our real sisters.

For most of us, for nine out of ten women with whom I talked, sisterhood is not a dream at all. Sisterhood is painful, incomplete, and occasionally humiliating. It is marred by distrust, disapproval, rejection, bitterness, envy, jealousy, despair, and hatred.

Sisterhood is marked by fierce love.

Looking at biological sisters, we understand what is equally true, but far more concealed, among female friends. We understand the coexistence of hate and love, cooperation and rivalry, generosity and selfishness. Looking at sisters, we apprehend ambivalence.

As a species, we don't like ambivalence. We like clear-cut, simple statements. We like to know where we stand, and who stands with us.

However, what we like and what we have in real life with our sisters directly contradict each other. Here are some statements made by sisters about each other.

"Everything I've ever done is what she couldn't do," says Noreen, twenty-two, older sister by two years.

"I was the pretty and dumb one, she was smart and plain." This is Melissa, twenty-four, honor student and younger sister by two years.

"This is really awful to say. When I had breast cancer, and my sister was absolutely wonderful, I looked into her eyes and I just knew that secretly, she was pleased she was finally the stronger one," Eunice, fifty-seven, older sister by four years, admits.

"I remember the events of my sister's life much more vividly than my own life: her graduation, her wedding, her trips to Europe, her picture on the living room piano," Margaret, forty-six, younger sister by four years, remarks.

"I've always admired and respected her. She was my ideal. You can imagine how I felt when she told me, just recently, that she wonders what it would have been like to have had a sister," says Carol, forty-one, younger sister by five years.

"Basically, I was afraid to compete with her. She was our father's favorite. She went to law school. I became a nurse when I wanted to be a doctor." This is from Madeleine, forty-nine, younger sister by two years.

"Now I realize that I used her life as a vicarious experience. She was wild; I was careful. But our parents rewarded me, while they punished her," Devon, fifty-one, older sister by four years, says.

"I've blocked it all out. I can't remember anything about living with her when we were children, except once I pushed her down the stairs, and once I tried to pour coffee on her. I feel too guilty to remember anything else," Laura, forty-three, older sister by four years, contributes.

The last comment is my own. I have indeed blocked out much of the childhood I shared with my younger sister. Even today, I attempt with great hesitation and real trepidation to remember our early lives. Remembering interferes with my dream of sisterhood and makes me suspicious of the friendships I value, of the friends I love, of my own vulnerability.

Remembering frightens me. I don't want to know, again, the "real" self who spent years terrorizing the little girl who seemed to get all the attention. I want to wipe out both of us.

Evidence that the dream of sisterhood *is* a dream is overwhelming. Nearly every one of the dozens of women with whom I talked revealed significant distress about her sister.

Fundamentally, sisterhood in our society seems to be based on disturbance—emotional, psychological, metaphorical, and literal. Most sisters find sisterhood very difficult.

Lewis Thomas is a medical doctor who thinks and writes about the connections between nature and human life. He has noticed that many invertebrates carry markings to attract compatible species. He is fascinated by symbiotic relationships, where the survival of one organism is impossible without the other. But these organisms are not two halves of one whole—they are not "co-addicts." Instead, they are separate but connected others. They form a relationship of perfect mutuality. Each gives what it has in order to get what it needs.

Human psychologists disapprove of such symbiosis. They believe that when two human beings draw that close to each other, they are no longer whole or complete. They become part people. But we don't need psychologists to tell us that too much closeness between two people is a problem. On our own we sense that something is radically wrong.

Seeing such a couple gives us an eerie, creepy feeling. Part of it originates in disgust. We are repelled by what we think is weakness. What if one died? What then? The sight of too much closeness makes us feel that our own independence, our unique specialness, and our ability to survive alone are endangered.

Yet at the same time we also feel something else: envy. We yearn for such closeness. We long to give what we have and get what we need. Our independence frightens us. "We hanker for friends."

Our society teaches us to prize independence and separation. But, simultaneously, we are surrounded by contrary messages. Most of the songs on the radio, most of our literature, and nearly every film we see provokes in us the desire to lose our separateness, to find union.

Sometimes it's called love. Sometimes it's called family. Sometimes it has no name. Sometimes it's just a picture, like the final scene in *Casablanca*—two men, buddies, walking into the fog together, sharing a complete sympathy beyond words and beyond the rules of civilization that tell us to be separate. The Lone Ranger and Tonto, Butch Cassidy and the Sundance Kid, Ishmael and Queequeg, Huckleberry Finn and Jim.

More recently, because of the feminist movement, this picture even has included women. Bette Midler and Shelley Long on stage at the end of *Outrageous Fortune*, the women in Fay Weldon's novels and Grace Paley's short stories, even Virginia Woolf, who wrote that "Chloe and Olivia shared a laboratory."

Still, the pictures of sympathetic union between women are hard to find. Strangely, since we assume that women bond with each other far more easily than men do, closeness between women makes us more uneasy than intimacy among men.

Instead, Lucy Ricardo and Ethel Mertz represent the sort of "sisters" who make us comfortable. Lucy dominant, Ethel her eternal second banana; a friendship based on a careful balance of power to keep them separate enough so that Ricky and Fred always come first, always come between.

Unlike Lucy and Ethel, Isobel and Betty Ingalls, described by Jeanne Marie Laskas, are sisters who have decided not to fear their intimacy.

Identical twins, Isobel and Betty married identical twin

brothers. At the age of fifty-nine, they live in identical houses next door to each other, filled with identical furniture. They wear identical clothing, makeup, hairdos, and glasses, and occasionally complete each other's identical sentences.

Isobel and Betty revel in their "we-ness." They like and admire each other. They offer each other constant, continual support.

But early in their marriages, the two sisters did heed advice to define themselves separately. "Everyone told us we were grown up and married now so we shouldn't dress alike. And so we conferred very carefully and tried not to," remembered Isobel. "It was awful," Betty added. Now, said Isobel, "We don't care if people think it's unusual or odd that we dress alike. That's really not our problem. That's everybody else's problem."

Isobel and Betty decided to define themselves by becoming the same. Their decision is fascinating, exactly as research describing the lives of identical twins fascinates most of us.

While we are repelled by their sameness, we yearn for their closeness. They have what we all want: a perfect and enduring community. Much as we would like to believe otherwise, Isobel and Betty enhance, rather than diminish, each other's life.

This would not surprise Lewis Thomas. He writes in *The Medusa and the Snail*, "We do not have solitary, isolated creatures. It is beyond our imagination to conceive of a single form of life that exists alone and independent, unattached to other forms. . . . Everything here is alive thanks to the living of everything else."

Yet, when my friends and I have dinner, when we owe

our lives to each other, we become somehow uneasy. Sometimes we go out of our way—far, far out in a direction that gives us no pleasure and ends in the icy reaches of sad loneliness—to insist that our community is accidental.

We laugh about it, but we resign ourselves without much argument when our children call us "feminist terrorists." We make sure not to certify our group existence with a name that celebrates us.

Not infrequently, we bring to dinner lingering anxiety about husbands and children left at home, or guilt about work undone. Sometimes we even recognize our resistance. Sometimes it's hard to keep a straight face.

The feeling I have, that I hope my friends share, is that when we are together I am alive. They give me the sense that right now, right here, my life is happening.

I would sacrifice a lot for that feeling, but why should I have to? Why should any of us have to? Why is it that most of us believe that female friendships are purchased with borrowed money on borrowed time, just waiting for the mortgage to be foreclosed? Who holds that note? Why are we, even a little, ashamed that we love each other?

Sisterhood is a profound and significant metaphor in women's lives. The dream of sisterhood closely resembles the dream of love—my other half, my lost twin, myself complete. It is a dream of merger, total sympathy, trust, and acceptance. The pleasure I experience when I am with my friends feels like a homecoming.

But it is not a return; it is an invention. The reality is not at all like the dream.

### COMPETITION BETWEEN SISTERS: YOU FIT INTO ME

The sibling bond gives us our first real experience of community, yet when we think of sisters, we think of rivals. The Latin word *rivalis* can mean "having rights to the same stream." For reasons connected to our family history, our literature, and our social mythology, when we think of sisters, we think of competition.

During the past twenty years, the sibling bond has been a fruitful field for research psychologists, but very little attention has been focused on sisters. In fact, the bond between sisters is nearly invisible in psychological literature. As is the case generally in psychoanalytic theory, sisters are thought about as *siblings*, or as versions of the theme played by brothers. However, the competition between sisters isn't conducted according to the same intrinsic model as the competition between brothers.

Psychologists tell us that siblings compete *against* each other in order to differentiate themselves and in order to gain parental attention, while they compete *for* each other in response to an external enemy.

Yet when brothers differentiate, they also challenge each other to meet some ideal standard. In the fairy tales about brotherly competition, for example, two brothers learn about honor and integrity in a competition with the third, usually youngest, brother. But when sisters compete, in fairy tales and real life, their differentiation does not lend either of them integrity. Unlike brothers, neither sister becomes, because of the competition, a complete person.

Instead, sisters compete to become part people—pretty and dumb, plain and smart, artistic and creative, sensible and practical. Take, for example, Virginia Woolf and Vanessa Bell, the Stephens sisters. Virginia, as most of us know, wrote novels of unsurpassed beauty and genuine wisdom, but she suffered all her life from feelings of insecurity and inferiority, particularly in relation to Vanessa, older than Virginia by two and one-half years. Vanessa, according to Virginia's internal mythology, was the beautiful sister, the sister who was really creative, whose success in life was reflected by her paintings, her marriage and romantic liaisons, her three children.

In comparison, Virginia, hungry for children, felt sterile, uncreative, awkward, and plain—this, despite objective evidence offered by the beautiful face captured in photographs as well as her magnificent novels and powerful, forceful political essays and literary criticism.

Virginia Woolf and Vanessa Bell were loving sisters. Tacitly, they agreed to develop themselves in a way precluding open competition between them. Virginia did not paint; Vanessa did not write seriously. In order to define themselves as different, they chose different arenas in which to excel.

Their relationship is reflected in fairy tales about sister pairs. In fairy tales, sisters are either polar opposites or complementary dyads, either Cinderella and her stepsisters or Snow White and Rose Red. Sisters in fairy tales either have nothing at all in common, or they fit together like two pieces of a jigsaw puzzle gone astray.

Margaret Atwood has written a very short poem about fitting together:

> You fit into me,
> Like a hook into an eye.
>
> A fish hook.
> An open eye.

So might sisters like Virginia Woolf and Vanessa Bell feel. The way even complementary sisters are encouraged to develop, the way they carefully learn not to compete with each other, can be lethal to both. Like "the fish hook and the open eye," for complementary sisters differentiation really means entanglement.

And even the most loving sisters know that we do not want to be either Snow White or Rose Red—we want to be both.

When sisters, like brothers, form their bond against an external antagonist, things are easier. Life is happier.

Here, for example, we can think about Jane Austen's *Pride and Prejudice*. Elizabeth and Jane Bennet are loving sisters, particularly because their mother is so difficult. Their father is not much good, either, isolating himself in his study to get away from his wife, offering comfort to his daughters only insofar as they join him in patronizing their mother.

Elizabeth and Jane turn to each other for strength, comfort, compassion, nurturing, and companionship. Even though Jane is beautiful and sweet while Elizabeth is witty and intelligent, they are the best of friends. Neither sister devalues the other according to the hierarchy established by their mother. They don't compete because neither wants her mother's attention—they mother each other.

However, when sisters actively compete for parental attention and love, things can get very bloody. In Jane Austen's *Persuasion* Anne Elliot, the middle one of three sisters, is scorned openly by her older sister in a contest for their father's love. Austen knew that this sort of competition was bad for both sisters. Although Anne is defeated, and therefore depressed, losing leaves her free to develop her mind and imagination. Elizabeth, the winner, is forced by her victory to become her father's surrogate wife, conforming her sexual and creative growth to satisfy his demands.

*Persuasion*, like several of Austen's novels, is a version of the Cinderella story. According to Bruno Bettelheim, "Cinderella" is the fairy tale most representative of sibling rivalry, but although Bettelheim accurately understands the overall tale, he omits the fact that these siblings are sisters. Like *Persuasion*, the Cinderella story teaches women that competition between sisters makes them miserable. In contrast to Austen's novel, however, in the fairy tale it's the noncompetitive sister who wins her father's love, although the father is disguised as a prince.

Yet Cinderella, like Elizabeth Elliot, loses her freedom. We do not doubt that her unknown surname changes to the prince's, that her ideas and ideals are molded by him, and that her sexuality is defined by him. Winning the competition with her stepsisters means Cinderella loses herself.

When brothers compete with each other for their father's approval, they really compete for inheritance. They compete to be the son who carries on the father's name and authority. But sisters who compete for their father compete for *disinheritance*—forfeiting personal authority in order to become what a man wants them to be. Sometimes it's very hard to be the favorite daughter.

Competition between sisters for their mother's attention and love can be equally terrible. This is the competition that Bettelheim missed in his analysis of "Cinderella."

Cinderella's story is a patriarchal fairy tale. Competition between Cinderella and her stepsisters for their mother is not at issue. Instead, Cinderella and her stepsisters compete for the fairy godmother's love. With her help, Cinderella wins the prince. Without her, the stepsisters, whatever they may do, remain ugly and unlovable.

Like Cinderella and her stepsisters, when real sisters compete for their mother, they compete for a magical, idealized mother, like Cinderella's fairy godmother. But because this is a patriarchal tale, when a sister wins her mother, she wins confinement. It can be as dangerous for women to win Mother as to win Father.

Being Mother's favorite means being *like* Mother. Winning Mother means taking care of her. Defeating your sister means that your life is the standard by which Mother's life is evaluated.

In Mary's family, she won her mother in a competition with her older sister, Grace. But Grace left home to work in New York City, while Mary remained in the small town where they had both grown up, raising her own family in a house only two blocks away from her mother.

"We're very close," said Mary about her relationship with her mother, "but sometimes I find myself really resenting Grace. She leads such an active life, while I'm surrounded by kids and diapers. And if Mother has any problem at all, I'm the one who has to be there to help her. I really dread what will happen as she gets older. Sometimes I feel I don't have any life of my own at all."

The crucial problem experienced by sisters in patriarchal families lies in our assumption that sisters inevitably and naturally compete with each other. Their community is defined by their competition.

Yet it *is* a community. When I think about Cinderella's story now, for example, I realize that I envy her stepsisters. They shared each other's clothes, combed each other's hair, witnessed each other's lives. Their open competition, the only way they were allowed to relate to each other, was a form of love.

Read through the stepsisters' perspective, the tale is about a sister bond created to combat an external antagonist—Cinderella. For the stepsisters, the wicked stepmother was a fairy godmother. She loved them both, treated them equally, and promoted their welfare. But because supporting them meant that she had to support their access to a man, they came to see each other as rivals.

Most sisters feel like stepsisters with each other. They feel as if one of them were Cinderella and the other were *both* of her stepsisters.

Bruno Bettelheim's omission is critical for women. Like the fairy tale, his analysis erases the real sister bond, the one between sisters in a patriarchal society. In the competition between sisters, winner and loser are two faces of the same person.

Mary, who envies her sister Grace's active professional life, acknowledges that according to Grace, she, Mary, was the winner. "Even though we're grown up, Grace still is jealous of me. She still says that Mother always loved me more, and she still can be very nasty to me. I guess neither of us made a real choice about our lives. If we had, we probably wouldn't feel so crummy about each other."

Grace and Mary fit into each other, a fish hook and an open eye.

## THE BLOOD BOND: DISAGREEMENT AND CONTINUITY AMONG SISTERS AND FRIENDS

When sisters grow up, they choose their female friends very carefully. They choose other women who feel like the sisters they never had. They choose against stepsisterhood.

They choose against the open competition they endured with their biological sisters. They push their competition with their sisters away, out of sight and out of mind.

However, the destructive competition women experienced with their sisters doesn't really go away. It returns in the way friends behave with each other.

Thinking about my own friends, I realize that a pattern emerges. A very good friend usually became a mere acquaintance in five or so years. Sometimes she became even less. I realize that my life is littered with women I no longer know, or see, or talk to, women with whom I once shared intimate conversations and intimate life.

Now, in my forties, I am no longer willing to accept that pattern. I want the friends now in my life to be there in ten, twenty, and thirty years. I want us to continue.

I want us to give up the dream of sisterhood. I want us to become real "sisters."

How will we do that? We seem to have no adequate model. The open competition we all experienced with our biological sisters has scared us. We don't know how to disagree.

Disagreement seems to be the key when sisters compete. In a way, sisters split up their mother's life. Each sister develops into an alternative version of Mother.

One sister may become like Mother, doing what she does, sharing her pleasures, her tastes, her dislikes, marrying the same sort of man, raising children in the same way. The other sister may actualize, in her life, choices her mother didn't make—not marrying, experiencing her mother's distastes as her own desires.

However, sisters rarely will experience their choices as different but equal. Instead, each competes for the "right" version, yet both alternatives are laden with meaning. Each, in a different way, celebrates their mother.

The problem is that open competition between sisters only appears to be open. In reality, it is a superficial competition, fought to gain superficial ends. The real competition, the one about each sister's right to exist, is just as secret as the competition between female friends.

What sisters really know is that they can fight with each other because they will always be sisters: they have a blood bond. But because sisters believe that their relationship will continue forever, they rarely learn how to resolve their competition. They rarely acknowledge that their competition represents the tension of disagreement, of differences that could be resolved even as new differences emerge.

Most of us know that the blood bond we share with our sisters is not enough. Forever is not enough. Forever doesn't ease present distress, anticipated rejection, accumulated grievances. While most sisters give each other love, few sisters *like* each other.

Instead, we like our friends. Often, too, we love our friends, but we choose friends we can like as we do not like our sisters.

We choose friends with similar values and styles, similar concerns and similar lives. We choose to like friends who tacitly confirm our own choices, friends with whom we will not compete.

In fact, most of us expect our friends not to compete with us. We confuse loyalty with agreement. While loyalty between sisters is the blood bond they share, loyalty between friends is a matter of conscious decision and commitment.

Caren, twenty-three, told me a story about loyalty between sisters. She remembered that when she was sixteen and her sister eighteen, her sister rushed out of their house one night to open the door of the car in which Caren sat "making out" with her date.

"She was absolutely white with anger," Caren said. "I guess I should tell you that this guy, my date, had dated her the year before. She *said* she was concerned for me because he was such a pig, but I knew that she wanted to kill me for taking him away from her."

Seven years later, Caren can laugh about this incident. "My sister's married now. I suppose I never should have dated her boyfriend, but it didn't seem like such a big deal at the time. I guess we agreed, without saying so, to forget about it."

Did Caren's sister forgive her? What else could she do? They're sisters. They share parents, anniversaries, and history. They will come home to the same house for the holidays. Their loyalty is part of their lives. And so is their anger.

Friends, however, can leave each other. Friends will not forgive the sort of competition sisters practice routinely with each other, so their anger is far more dangerous.

Friends believe that anger interferes with loyalty, as do disagreement and competition.

Looking at my history with my own friends, I realize that relationships began to dwindle at the point when our differences appeared. We seemed to feel that we could no longer like each other if we were different. Indeed, when our differences emerged we acted more like biological sisters than in "sisterhood." We did to each other what we longed to do to our real sisters—we left each other.

## THE MIRROR CRACK'D: SISTERS AND IDENTITY

The emotional issues that make it difficult to tolerate difference in our friends are based in our own conceptions of ourselves.

When we look in our friends' eyes, we want to see ourselves reflected as we are at our best. We do not want that mirror cracked to reveal our "real" selves, the ones our sisters know so well.

Psychologists tell us that as we grow, three levels of self develop, sequentially. The first, and most primary, is the core identity, formed in early childhood in relation to the people in our families. Core identity defines us as smart or dumb, generous or selfish, passive or active, sociable or solitary.

The philosopher-psychologist William James believed that our core identity was the "truest, strongest, deepest self." We may like it, we may loathe it, but rarely will we reveal it to anyone other than our psychiatrists and, of course, our siblings. Since our core was formed when we lived with our siblings, they know it, sometimes far too well.

Later, in middle childhood and throughout adolescence, we create a subidentity. We take the personalities formed when we were small children and put them to good or bad use. We actively develop special talents or we passively wait for life to tell us what those talents are. We think of ourselves as athletes, intellectuals, Republicans or Democrats, popular or shy. When we form our subidentities, we consciously choose to be who we are. Subidentity is not as crucial to our sense of self as the core identity; we can change it as we develop. It offers us a way to identify ourselves to other people. Sometimes, even siblings know us only at the level of subidentity. Particularly when there is a large age gap between siblings, or when, for one reason or another, siblings grow up in separate households, they know us more by subidentity than by core.

By the end of adolescence we develop a persona. Now we can be who we are while at the same time we pretend we are someone else. Erving Goffman used the term *persona*, coined by Jung, to define the way we all learn to perform and dramatize in order to create impressions on those around us.

For example, we learn to disguise a desire for solitude under a mask of social chatter, to conceal shyness by developing social competence. We learn to show the world only those characteristics we admire and respect. At least we hope we do.

Drs. Stephen Bank and Michael Kahn, who developed this concept of the three-tiered self, also tell us in *The Sibling Bond* (page 60) that "one's core self, seen through the eyes of a sibling, or *compared* with that of a sibling, remains as one essential reference point for personal identity."

In other words, at least part of a core identity defining us as dumb and pretty has to do with a sibling defined in *her* core as plain and smart. It is because siblings retain a lifelong knowledge of each other's core that they can seem so dangerous to each other. Each, for the other, represents the threat of unmasking. Each can, at any time, expose the other, can reveal the "truth" of the other.

Sisters, especially, feel very vulnerable to threats of unmasking. Since so much of traditional feminine life is lived behind a series of masks, exposure seems to evoke fears of annihilation as well as humiliation. Only a sister remembers us as we really are: a fat, dirty, greedy, malicious, domineering, bossy little girl.

Only a sister can compare the sleek body that now exists with the chubby body hidden underneath. Only a sister knows about former pimples, failing math, and underwear kicked under the bed.

And we don't trust our sisters not to tell "the truth." We don't trust them not to take sweet revenge by revealing the little girls we would rather keep very, very secret.

Yet, more often than not, the "truth" sisters know about each other has very little to do with reality. It is a truth manufactured by their family.

For example, Victoria, forty-four, remembers that during their childhood, photographs of her older sister Megan filled their parents' house. "Megan was the beautiful one; she had the perfect hair, perfect nose, perfect large brown eyes. I was the mess. There were no pictures of me anywhere," said Victoria, whose own dark hair and small features combine to make her quite beautiful.

Recently Victoria visited Megan. She found that her sister, still heeding their parents, had filled her own apartment with photos of herself. And even standing beside her, even able to compare herself to the sister who, in reality, resembles her quite closely, Victoria still felt like a "mess."

"This is foolish, I know," Victoria continued. "There was one picture in particular, a large glossy eight-by-ten, that made her appear so stunning I could barely stand to look at it. But in fact, on the day I visited, Megan looked about as much like the face in the photo as I did. We were both overworked and tired, neither of us had makeup on, and we were both wearing jeans and sweatshirts. But the photo seemed to be *her*, while she almost seemed like someone I didn't know."

To Victoria, the "truth" overwhelmed reality. The core identities each sister had been given by their parents had become articles of faith for both women. Megan was beautiful. Victoria was plain.

In our society, we are very fond of hierarchies. When we can understand anything by locating it in categories from one to ten, we feel secure. We know we're getting what we paid for: we know where we stand.

The hierarchy of the three-tiered self makes us comfortable. As a model, it allows us to chart our development and quantify our progress. It fits in well with what psychologists call "stage theory," the idea that our lives move through predictable, measurable stages. As long as we can predict them, the changes in our lives don't frighten us so much.

But the reality of change, like the reality of the three-tiered self, is not at all so smoothly predictable. For one thing, the three-tiered-self idea proposes that our development is progressive. First core, then subidentity, then persona. No overlapping, no confusion, no moving two steps forward only to fall back four.

Lewis Thomas writes that "having more than one self is supposed to be deeply pathological . . . [but] it is the simultaneity of their appearance that is the real problem." Thomas means that we are comfortable and happy when the self we were at age five is gone by the time the self we are at age fifteen appears, and so on throughout our lives. Our belief in a "core self" has more to do with our need to believe that we are unified than with reality.

We all realize how different we are now than we ever were before. Sometimes, a forty-year-old person looks back at a twenty-year-old self and is staggered by its foolishness, or, even worse, mourns its lost vitality. Men, in particular, tend to idealize their adolescent selves, when all of life seemed possible, before bills, mortgages, children, and wives closed in.

On the one hand, we hate change. We resist it by insisting that who we are now is a predictable, inevitable development from who we were then. We want to think of ourself as a coherent, unified individual.

So we believe our current identity conceals inside a core that never changes, a core containing whatever is "real" about us. On the other hand, what we believe denies our own development, denies the fact that most people can and do change.

When sisters look into each other's eyes and see the mirror reflecting their "core," they really see only the little girls they once were. They do not see the women they have become.

Ultimately, the people we are result from all the choices, conscious and unconscious, that we make in our lives.

In reality, most sisters share only a small portion of each other's lives. But since that portion, during childhood, was so powerful emotionally, often it seems that who we are depends on who our sisters are not. Often, sisters carry each other around inside themselves for the rest of their lives. No matter how geographically distant, a sister can remain the touchstone we use for our own identity.

But getting to know my sister now that we are both adults has taught me about the core self. It's taught me that when sisters compete to become part people, when we compete fiercely for differentiation, we develop negative versions of what could be positive qualities.

For example, in my own family, older sisters were given lots of authority, but because we were two, my authority developed in contrast to my sister's subordination. Instead of understanding authority in terms of self-control, then, I came to confuse it with authoritarian behavior, with control *over* someone else: my sister. Further, instead of understanding her quietness as calm self-control, I perceived my sister as shy and submissive.

Now I think that when we who are sisters look at each other, we see the positions we occupied in our childhood families. We see what amounts to job descriptions: older sister—determined, temperamental, bossy, outgoing, popular, ambitious; younger sister—stable, passive, shy, noncompetitive. I fantasize that our parents placed unconscious advertisements in the "help wanted" section of some newspaper in the sky, published by family history, written on stone tablets.

As it has turned out, my sister and I resemble each other much more than we differ from each other. Our genetic inheritance and shared family life make us look alike and account for similar senses of humor as well as the way we walk and talk.

For me, giving up the need to think of my sister as unalterably different—worse in some ways, better in others—was like Dumbo giving up his magic feather. I discovered I could fly on my own.

I discovered that my "core" self was not a core at all, and that I am sociable mainly with women younger than I am, and shy with just about everyone else. What was even harder to realize was that authority meant self-possession. I learned I could be self-directed without needing to offer advice to other people, particularly to younger women. I learned that being authoritative was a strength as long as I remembered not to use it as a weapon.

*       *       *

When sisters accept the notion of a core self, we also accept unnecessary restriction and limitation. We accept life as partial people. We accept the sort of competition that permits only one version of our mother's life to survive.

Sisters can make each other feel crazy. When we are together as adults, all the selves we once were and are now exist simultaneously. We look at each other with "memory bank" eyes, so, in order to feel sane and in control, we unconsciously agree to erase our multiple selves, relating to each other only through the "core" self.

Although I'm sure my sister cannot realize it, because it's all she has ever seen of me, I am far less domineering when we are not together. And I assume she is far less passive.

Our self—our selves—is a response to our social and physical environment. We create our selves using the tools of innate temperament, intelligence, self-determination, will, and how our childhoods affected all of these. I no longer believe that there is a core—or at least not only one. There are multiple alternatives, of which we are guided by parents, schools, and circumstance to choose one, long before we know we have choice.

But the choices we make change as we grow, as our physical, intellectual, and emotional resources develop. The mirror our sisters hold up for us—and we for them— reflects only one of those choices, made at one time, not the "truth" for all time.

## TEN LITTLE INDIANS: SIBLING ORDER AND PERSONALITY

It is very hard to give up feeling that we are who we were with our childhood sisters. In truth, we retain throughout our lives qualities we developed early on.

Thus it is very important to know something about the personalities older and younger sisters develop with each other. It helps us know ourselves, it helps us understand why we do what we do, and it helps us change.

The branch of sibling research that possesses an almost eerie capacity to predict behavior is sibling order. Psychologists and sociologists who work on sibling order believe that our personalities and life choices are related directly to the positions we occupied in our original families.

Walter Toman, whose book *Family Constellations* marked out this field nearly thirty years ago, even includes advice on how sibling order will affect our response to marriage. For example, Toman believes that older sisters of brothers should marry younger brothers of sisters. Older sisters of sisters will also do better with younger brothers of brothers. Since older siblings generally have greater authority in their original families, while younger sisters and brothers are well trained in submission, such combinations produce "compatible" relationships.

When two younger siblings marry, the balance of power also remains intact, but the couple will have difficulty making decisions. How will they ever decide what car or house to buy, or how many children to have, when each expects the other to take the lead?

Two older siblings who marry are in even more trouble. Each can make a decision, all right, but neither knows about concession. *They* will need two houses and two cars.

And, to further paraphrase Toman's work, only children should be drowned at birth. Since they never learned about sharing and cooperation through interaction with siblings, they will be impossible as spouses.

Oversimplified, Toman's work becomes funny. We all know many couples composed of two older or two younger siblings who are just fine together, and more recent research on only children, in fact, directly contradicts Toman's material.

Taking a comprehensive look at single-child families, Ellie McGrath demonstrates that an only child can become a strong, motivated, creative individual, capable of deep and lasting relationships, precisely because only children have never experienced competition for parental attention and love. They assume cooperation at times when adults who grew up vying with siblings expect competition. But when we think about sibling-order theories in a more complicated way, they become more difficult to dismiss.

For example, my mother was the youngest daughter and last child of a mother who was herself the older in a family of two sisters.

Although my mother's family included brothers as well as one older sister, she and her sister were a pair within the larger sibling unit. Most siblings in large families pair off, forming dyads based on closeness of age, shared personal characteristics, the same gender, or an alliance based on their parents' tacit directions to think of each other that way.

My mother thus became very definitely a younger sister. Both her older sister and her mother—another older sister—were entrenched firmly in older-sister personalities. They were bossy, creative, commanding, critical, verbal, curious, competitive, and ambitious. They were the responsible ones.

In contrast, my mother is cautious, subtle, indirect, insecure, submissive, artistic—and if not at all irresponsible, she tends to distrust her own judgment when faced with a louder, older, female voice.

I was my mother's first daughter. Unconsciously, when I

was born, she gave me the authority she had been taught oldest daughters deserve. Just as she was a little afraid of my grandmother and aunt, she became a little afraid of me. Like them, I became bossy and authoritative, particularly toward my younger sister.

When my sister was born, my mother relaxed. Here was a child she understood: like her, the younger sister of a sister. She could teach her how to survive with an older sister. She knew intuitively how my sister felt about the world. Their relationship always seemed to me easier than mine with my mother. They shouted less at each other, agreed more, were happier together. I thought she was the favorite—I was the stepchild.

I now recognize how much my mother loved us both. However, my sister, developing according to family direction into a younger sister, made my mother more comfortable. Had my mother been an older sister, the opposite could as easily have been the result.

When I married for the first time, I chose an older brother of brothers. We were exactly the kind of couple for whom Walter Toman predicts disaster. Nevertheless, although that marriage did end fourteen years after it began, I believe that it was not destroyed by the fact that we were two older siblings—at least not altogether. Instead, I can now see that when I married, I chose a man who would be my older sister. I envied my sister her comfortable, apparently easy, relationship with my mother. I wanted it for myself.

Changing sibling position is not easy. Despite what I desired, I discovered that I really didn't like being a younger sister. I really didn't like being passive and submissive, trading an identification as an authority for one where I listened to someone else.

I discovered I wanted to be both an older and a younger sister, sometimes at the same time. I wanted to be sometimes strong and sometimes weak, sometimes a clown and sometimes serious, sometimes responsible and sometimes dependent. I learned that in order to be both sisters, I would have to "sister" myself.

Like most older sisters, I had spent very little time reflecting on my relationship with my sister. Younger sisters tell a different story.

In general, the younger sisters with whom I talked revealed, one after another, how significant and important their older sisters were to them. For example, Amy, forty-four, reported that she noticed whenever she and her friend Pam get together, they talked about their older sisters.

"When Pam and I are together, it can sound like we're obsessed with our sisters, although I don't talk about mine as much when I'm with friends who are not younger sisters," said Amy. "In my experience, when younger sisters get together it's like we heave a sigh of relief—now we can talk about our sisters in ways that we each understand, and we don't have to apologize for boring each other."

Younger sisters unconsciously believe, sometimes obsessively, that another woman always precedes them. Whatever they may do, she has done first. For many younger sisters, this sense of "secondness" gives them the feeling that they are life's losers, defeated in any competition before they enter. Often, in fact, younger sisters respond to feelings of envy evoked by another woman's accomplishments with a sense of sick despair. Envy signals to them that they are called to enter a competition they can't possibly win.

In contrast, older sisters often identify envious feelings

as a challenge to compete. Unlike their younger sisters, they see themselves as capable and competent. When they envy another woman, they see no reason they should not have what she possesses.

At the same time, older sisters fear their younger sisters. This is real news for younger sisters, who have spent most of their lives afraid of their powerful and larger older sisters. Older sisters are scared that younger sisters will call in the debt of their freedom.

They fear that their younger sisters, if they asked them, would tell them how domineering, how authoritarian, how privileged, they are. Older sisters fear that their younger sisters' words will tip the balance of guilt they carry into an unbearable burden, and they don't want to hear those words.

Younger sisters fear their older sisters' words differently. They fear that the voice they heard too much when they were children will once again become a powerful force in their adult lives, and that once again they will hear how small, incompetent, and inferior they are. When younger sisters choose each other as friends, they choose a bond to affirm the shaky self-esteem they believe their older sisters did their damnedest to destroy.

Yet whether they are older or younger, sisters rarely realize that the relationship they shared with each other profoundly affects their relationships with other women.

I realized the significance of sister relationships several years ago, when I attended a seminar conducted by Jean Baker Miller and her colleagues, members of the Stone Center at Wellesley College. In the course of the week-long workshop, Miller and her colleagues asked the fifty women attending to divide themselves into two discussion groups, later to be reintegrated as a larger unit.

The groups were labeled "mothers" and "daughters." Those of us who joined the "mother" group went outside to sit on the lawn; those of us who were "daughters" took possession of the seminar room.

I joined the "mothers." Once we were gathered outside, we shared more information about ourselves. Not surprisingly, all of us in this group, some twenty-five women, were mothers, and most of us were mothers of daughters. But that was not all we were. We discovered that each woman who chose to join the "mother" group was an older sister—every one of us, no exceptions. And we realized that returning inside to join the "daughter" group provoked in us an almost palpable anxiety. We thought they would yell at us.

They did. When we rejoined the "daughter" group, the room was filled with hostility, despite the fact that during the two days preceding this exercise we had formed ourselves into a large and supportive community. The "daughter" group, it turned out, was composed of younger sisters. Yet many of the women in the "daughter" group were mothers of daughters, just like the women in the "mother" group. However, in choosing to identify as either "mother" or "daughter," we all unconsciously acted on our sibling position, rather than on our very conscious parental status.

We quickly became aware that being mothers and daughters somehow counted less than being older or younger sisters *when we choose a group of women where we felt we "belonged."*

Many of the women I interviewed for this book reported feeling the same way. When they thought about their close friends, they realized that the majority of them occupied the same sibling position. Older sisters chose other older sisters as friends, younger sisters tended to become intimate with other younger sisters.

Although psychological research directs us to think about women almost exclusively in terms of the mother/daughter relationship, adult women form relationships with each other based on their sibling positions.

This information brings us back to where the feminists began. Women choose their friends for "sisterhood."

## INTIMACY AND JUDGMENT AMONG SISTERS AND FRIENDS

As we have seen, "sisterhood" in friendships and families is a conflicted experience, in which women forge powerful bonds—both loving and hateful. "Sisters" can be the best of friends or the worst enemies.

This is important information for women. It allows us to understand who our friends are and why we chose them. It allows us to see that we choose our friends to confirm our view of the world—perspectives we developed as older and younger sisters. It also allows us to understand why the relationships with the men in our lives often seem so difficult, while our friendships seem so easy. Frequently the men we choose to love replicate the relationships we experienced with our sisters, *not* with our fathers and mothers.

For example, all too often, sisters are unable to talk to each other about their competition. Instead of a relationship based on disagreement and resolution, they are locked into one based on judgment and evaluation.

"I don't know how to tell her how I feel without her feeling judged," said Hallie, forty-nine, about her younger sister. "I want to say, 'You don't have to defend yourself;

we're different,' but something stops me. The words aren't there. And I guess my defensiveness is equally high."

Like Hallie, most of the sisters I talked to revealed that when they thought about their sisters, they judged them as they would not dream of judging their friends. Almost without exception, too, these were the same sorts of judgments they made about the men in their lives.

Libby, forty-seven, expressed it well. "When I'm at a party with my husband," she said, "at some level I expect the other people there to judge me according to how they perceive him. I've discovered that indirectly I monitor his behavior, watching to see whether he's being too loud or too quiet, whether he's offending anyone. I know this is wrong, but it's hard to let go of the feeling that when they react to him, they also wonder how I could have married someone like that."

Libby describes a confusion of identity shared by many women. Unlike men, as women grow up they are encouraged to form identities based on connection with other people. As Nancy Chodorow writes, women develop fluid, permeable ego boundaries. Women feel that who they are is connected intricately with the other people in their lives. While such connection can be a real strength, it also can be a liability in adult life.

Emotionally, we can feel joined at the hip to our husbands and children, and to our sisters. Our joint identities can make us feel that the actions and behavior, even the personalities, of our families tacitly comment on ourselves.

Yet at the same time, most women also believe that correcting a disturbed relationship with a sister means getting closer to her. We think that the problem is intimacy. We believe that intimacy means more, rather than less, closeness. However, when sisters get closer to each other, often they increase their secret judgments.

In contrast, genuine intimacy depends on knowing that another person is separate, really other. It depends on respecting another person's difference, on tolerating her faults because they belong to her, not to oneself.

Although it is very difficult to change our relationships with our sisters, knowing that *we* are judging *them* can have direct impact on relationships with husbands and lovers.

Sometimes, in fact, focusing on sister relationships produces unexpected illumination. For example, June, forty-five, told me how, after several years of bitter anger, she finally came to understand her relationship with her husband's former wife.

"I knew something was wrong—wrong with me," said June, "because I was the one who stayed so angry at Helene, long after Neil had let go. Finally, I realized that I was relating to Helene just like I had related to my own sister, putting Neil between us even though he was clear about his love and loyalty to me.

"I was the one who couldn't let go," June continued, "not until I could recognize that the hate I felt for Helene was a version of the anger I felt toward my sister. First, of course, I had to admit that I *was* so angry at my sister. Then I could recognize that it was the same emotion I felt toward Helene. I still feel it, but now I don't also feel so desperate about acting on it. When Neil talks to Helene now about the kids, I'm able to separate my feelings from the reality—the reality that he loves me, not her. In a funny way, now I feel like Helene is really my 'sister.' I don't think I'll ever love or even like her, but at least I'm able to accept her as part of the family."

\* \* \*

Sometimes, learning that the same personality that makes us comfortable makes our sister very *un*comfortable can be very important. For example, Ginny, forty-nine, older than her sister by two years, possesses all the characteristics of an older sister. She is an exceptionally outgoing woman, whose unusual competence, intelligence, and ambition have earned her a solid position at a major university. Ginny's husband, Ted, fifty-five, is an equally brilliant scientist, but, as a younger brother, is far more shy and solitary than his wife.

Ginny and Ted seem to have divided the human personality into separate spheres. Yet, unlike those in many apparently similar relationships, neither Ginny nor Ted is a part person.

When they go to a party, for instance, Ginny usually takes over, becoming the life and soul of the gathering. Ted, even after more than twenty-five years of marriage, loves her performance. He somehow doesn't feel erased by her, while she doesn't feel that his shyness casts a negative reflection on her.

Ginny believes that her loving relationship with Ted is at least partially due to understanding how her sister felt about her outgoing personality. As the older sister, Ginny learned very early that she could lead, that she loved to lead. But discovering that the sister she believed needed protection and advice did not at all feel the same way was very important.

"My sister Marie arrived at my college two years after I entered," said Ginny. "Until then, I thought we were very close. One day, I went to her room to see her, but before I could knock, I heard her voice inside, talking to one of her friends. And what she said absolutely shocked me. She was talking about me, about how bossy I could be, how loud, and making jokes about me.

"When I remember that moment I still feel tremendous pain and humiliation. Still, after more than thirty years, I feel betrayed. But at the same time, I'm very grateful I did overhear her. I know she never would have told me all those things—in fact, she hasn't, not to this day, and I've never told her I heard her say them.

"It made me think about who I was," Ginny continued. "It made me realize that qualities I valued in myself must be very hard for her to bear. And I also realized that quite a lot of my popularity had to do with bravado. Much of it, of course, I wouldn't want to change—I like entertaining people; I like practicing a sort of open warmth and generosity. And a lot of it I couldn't change, even if I wanted to. When I'm anxious, I automatically shift into a 'big sister' mode. I hide the fact that I'm feeling anxious by trying to make it my place and my party.

"But I also love my sister, and some of it I could change. Or at least I could be aware of how I affected other people. My sister gave me a great gift. I think that even though I married Ted because of all his wonderful qualities, so different from my own, if I hadn't overheard my sister I would have begun to disparage him exactly because he wasn't like me.

"Overhearing my sister allowed me to think—continually—about how Ted and I were different, and how that was good, not bad. I think we've been able to talk more over the years because of that shock I had from my sister. Since then, it's never been so hard to face myself."

Ginny realizes, ironically, that she was very lucky. Her luck circumvented the major difference between the way we generally relate to our friends and the way we relate to our sisters. Women who are friends suspend their judgments about each other. They are friends *because* they tolerate each other's occasional crankiness, irritability, foolishness, and difficult behavior. They focus on their pleasure in each other.

But sisters judge each other. They feel defined by each other; they often spend years trying to be different because they fear that other people will judge *them* as *they* judge their sisters.

Ironically, when sisters compete with each other for difference, they are competing to evade the judgments they themselves are making about each other. They are competing to not judge themselves. Psychologists call this dynamic projective identification, meaning that we see in other people all the qualities we loathe about ourselves.

We are more comfortable, emotionally and psychologically, when we can believe that the parts of ourselves we hate are not part of us at all. They belong to our sisters.

However, recognizing our own judgmentalism toward our sisters can have a profound effect on our relationships both with our sisters *and* with women who are not our sisters.

Ginny, for example, believes she became a feminist as she grew older because she was able to face her attitude toward her sister during a very formative period in her own life.

"Recognizing that Marie judged *me* made me realize how I was judging her. As I said before, I really am grateful. Because I also knew she loved me. That made it easier to take, and take in the right way.

"Marie and I are very different, but since that time I've worked hard not to disparage her difference. That has had a direct effect on my relationships with other women, both

friends and colleagues. I really can understand that I'm
rubbing some women the wrong way without thinking that
it must be all their fault. I've grown up to like other women
in a way I think would have been impossible if I had never
come to terms with my own need to judge."

## NO EXIT: MORALITY AND LOYALTY BETWEEN SISTERS AND FRIENDS

When we dream of "sisterhood," I no longer believe we are
thinking about our relationships with biological sisters.
Instead, relationships between adult sisters constitute a
trail, not a core. What sisters really see when they look at
each other is historical research. The competition between
adult sisters provides the most visible traces of the cauldron
in which they began to be formed.

The naturalist Loren Eiseley writes that when he goes
out to discover the "secret of life," he does so in the autumn. "Of late years," Eiseley says, "I have come to suspect
that the mystery may just as well be solved in a carved and
intricate seed case out of which life has flown, as in the seed
itself."

The competition between adult sisters, making each despair and often despise her sister, is exactly such a seed case.
It is the husk remaining of the intense life sisters once
shared. In it, as Eiseley writes, "there is an unparalleled
opportunity to examine in sharp and beautiful angularity
the shape of life, without its disturbing muddle of juices and
leaves." But it is the rare sister who can get enough emotional distance to realize she deals with a dry husk rather
than a raging volcano.

Maggie, forty-two, younger than her sister Maureen by
four years, described it well. "She hated me then and she
hates me now. She was always jealous. She always tried to

hurt me. Our father died about two years ago. Maureen was named executor of his estate. About six months ago, she called to tell me she had some of his things and that I could take my pick whenever I had time. So I went to her apartment, where she showed me a shopping bag filled with junk, stuff she should just have thrown away. In the meantime, looking around her apartment, I saw all the furniture and paintings my father had accumulated that we *should* have shared. When I asked about them, Maureen said that he would have wanted her to have them since I always was the favorite and got so much more when we were kids. I didn't know what to say at that point, except to feel that I never wanted to see her again."

The competition between adult sisters, no matter what age they are, keeps them their parents' children. It keeps their parents alive in the present, and it keeps the present in bondage to the past.

Sometimes the competition between sisters lasts only as long as their parents are alive. But for other sisters, their competition is all they feel toward each other. Giving it up would mean giving each other up.

At this point, the competition between sisters and the competition between friends becomes genuinely confused.

As I have explained elsewhere in this book, *all* the women I interviewed began our conversations with the statement that they did not compete with other women. While most of those women were able to think beyond that initial response, nearly all continued to insist that their competitiveness with other women did not exist in relationships with friends. They simply did not compete with their friends, nor did their friends compete with them.

This point seemed to be very important. The intensity of

their voices and their serious expressions told me that competition between female friends was far more significant than a simple fact of relationship; it was a point of honor, the equivalent of masculine insistence on courage or honesty. Like men admitting cowardice, women, when they faced their competitiveness toward their friends, felt their integrity was in question. They felt fragmented, as though they had failed to live up to an ideal of themselves they carried around in their imagination.

I wrote earlier that female friends talk to each other. But female friends don't merely chat; they pay attention. They describe their conversations using terms such as *being there*, *listening*, and *understanding*. For most women, conversation with their female friends is a moral act.

Carol Gilligan tells us in *Mapping the Moral Domain* (page 151) that for women, "the willingness and the ability to care become a source of empowerment and a standard of self-evaluation."

Care, for women, takes on a moral dimension. It signals our ability to perceive another person in her own terms and to respond to need. In contrast, the failure to care, or detachment, feels somehow immoral to most women. Women believe that when they "don't care," they are bad people—unethical and dishonorable. Since women are loyal to other people rather than to social institutions, not caring signals disloyalty.

In a way, we can think about competition between women, particularly women who are friends, as the stage on which women act out moral and ethical decisions.

The disloyalty most women associate with competition feels like a failed morality. That's why recognizing our competition with our friends is so painful. Loyal friends don't compete with each other, not simply out of emotional desire, but also from a deeply rooted perception of moral rightness. Ironically, this means that when biological sisters openly compete with each other, we fail each other morally and ethically. We demonstrate *disloyalty*.

Most sisters know this, however we may conceal the knowledge from ourselves and from our sisters. We know that the blood bond between us feels more like a facade of loyalty. We know it is not the real thing, the thing we dream of creating with our friends, but, even more ironically, the morality women associate with noncompetition does not belong to us. We have not created it.

Moral action inherently means self-determination. We act morally and ethically when we choose, with self-awareness and with consciousness of consequences, what we do. Women have not chosen noncompetition—it has been chosen for them.

In our society, there is a real division between the morality expected of men and the morality expected of women. Traditionally, women were not asked to demonstrate physical courage or adhere to a ritualized code of ethics. Instead, they were encouraged to practice "situational" ethics, making moral decisions based on human relationships, not impersonal standards of justice. Thus, most women developed an "ethic of care." For women, basing action on impersonal standards *feels* unethical and immoral.

However, this large division between men and women conceals the fact that women have not *chosen* to develop an ethic of care. It was formed by the traditional division of labor, aligning women with home and family, historically denying them access to public endeavor.

Especially now that Carol Gilligan's work allows us to realize how valuable is the ethic of care, it becomes even more difficult to recognize that it restricts women in the same way the ethic of justice restricts men. Through the ethic of care, women have developed intensely negative feelings about *not* caring. But women associate not caring with a wide variety of actions that can, in reality, produce "not-caring" behavior.

For example, when we link loyalty with noncompetition, we actually become disloyal. Our definition of loyalty is restricted to the narrow assumption that loyalty means agreement. Loyalty means no difference. When we refuse to compete with our friends, we really imply that we don't *trust* our friends to be different from us, nor do we trust ourselves to be loyal in the face of difference. Tacitly, we imply that we can be loyal only when our friends are like us.

In an ironic and terribly destructive way, many of us practice the morality of slaves and masters. Slaves always know more about their masters than masters know about slaves. Without complex information about masters, slaves would not survive their condition. Furthermore, slaves are certain—and right—that whatever information about them their masters possess will be used against them.

When we practice noncompetition with our friends, we unconsciously transfer into our relationships almost a parody of the master-slave relationship. When we don't tell our friends what we are really thinking, when we believe that competition signals disloyalty instead of disagreement, we act like slaves. When we fail to recognize our friends' difference and disagreement, when we assume that a competitive friend is no friend at all, we are masters.

Noncompetition as the basis for friendship conflicts with genuine friendship. Noncompetition means that we exclude *ourselves*—our own opinions, desires, and ideas—from our friendships. It is actually unethical: when we practice it, the connection between us is violated just as much as when we are excessively competitive—the fear we inherited from life with our biological sisters.

The way out of this dilemma for women is very difficult, but there is a way out, a way for us to *choose* our moral standard.

The answer is contained in work done by Albert Hirschman. Concerned about how people behaved in deteriorating organizations, Hirschman contrasted two strategies used for remedy: exit and voice.

Exit, exactly as the term implies, means that one leaves a sinking ship before going under with it. Exit is neat, clean, practical. It coincides with an ethic of justice supporting a consumer economy in which buyers are encouraged to switch from one product to another version made by a different company. When we use exit as a strategy for remedy, we do not stick around to try to change things.

In contrast, voice is messy, complicated, and personal. Hirschman writes that voice is located on a continuum "all the way from grumbling to violent protest." Using voice means that open, personal encounters are more valuable than private, secret, and impersonal action. Voice insists on community and on the sort of personal engagement inherently present in the concept of community. In terms of loyalty, voice operates to hold exit at bay. It enforces the loyalty of "hanging in there" in the face of disagreement and dissension.

People who use voice to solve problems in their relationships feel that real disloyalty is located in exit—leaving too soon to work things out, running away, escaping.

Biological sisters believe that exit is *impossible*, but that belief does not make them loyal to each other. Their blood bond does not mean they seek to "hang in there," insisting that things change. In fact, it can mean quite the reverse. Our society is the only one in history that has ever presented exit as a possible solution to family life.

We teach our children that the place in which they grow up may not be the location of their adult lives. Our highly mobile society encourages a fantasy of escape from one's family. However, no matter how far we travel geographically, most of us discover that exit is an illusion. We carry our families around inside us as the yardstick of our development. We are more intensely responsive to mothers, fathers, brothers, and sisters hundreds or thousands of miles away than we are to our next-door neighbors, but maintaining the illusion of exit permits sisters to continue unresolved competitions for their whole lives and to mistake the dynamic that destroys them for the tie that binds them together.

The illusion of exit, combined with their blood bond, permits sisters to believe that they don't need to talk to each other the way they talk to their friends. It allows sisters to make judgments about each other. It allows sisters to deny how much each has changed.

Even more significantly, the illusion of exit allows sisters to deny how *similar* they are. The competition most sisters experience is based on their perception that each must be different from the other: older or younger, fat or thin, artistic or pragmatic, smart or silly. As long as we pretend that exit can be the solution to our difference, while at the same time we believe that there is *no* exit from our blood bond, we are not able to face our real competition—the one based on how much alike we really are.

Friends, on the other hand, are fully aware of the dangers of exit as a solution to difference. Though friends may believe in voice, may believe that their relationship is based on hours and hours of talking to each other—in effect, many female friends, like sisters, don't talk to each other at all.

Often, the intimacy friends experience lasts only as long as "voice" doesn't get messy and complicated. Often, friends talk to each other only so long as they recognize how much like each other they are. When they meet difference—and competition—they exit.

Neither friends nor sisters are always able to "hang in there," but exit causes real trouble. Exit can produce life-shattering consequences: it can result in loneliness, misery, and isolation.

When exit is preferred to voice, our relationships are based on domination. Sometimes such domination is fairly visible. For instance, when a husband and wife conclude most of their arguments because one of them threatens to leave, the threatening partner dominates.

Sometimes, however, domination is not apparent to either friends or sisters. Rosemary and Annis, two sisters now in their fifties, demonstrate how subtle such domination can be.

Born five years apart, Rosemary and Annis grew up "competing about nearly everything," remembered Rosemary.

As they developed, they chose exit to solve what each understood as their irreconcilable difference. One went to college on the East Coast, the other on the West Coast.

While Annis, the older sister, focused on politics and public speaking, Rosemary, the younger, concentrated on painting and psychology. After each married, they lived thousands of miles apart. Nevertheless, their "nonrelation-

ship" profoundly affected their lives at a level neither sister
could possibly recognize.

When Rosemary was eighteen, in her first year at college, she became pregnant. Since she attended a school on
the opposite side of the country from where her older sister
then lived, getting pregnant seemed to have nothing to do
with her sister.

Rosemary understood her predicament as her own tragedy, understood dropping out of school and getting married as her own solution, and, when she had three more
babies before she was twenty-five, was baffled by the com-
plexity and difficulties of what seemed to be her own dis-
tressing life.

Meanwhile, Annis graduated from college, married, and
had one baby. She spent the next ten years of her life—
while her younger sister demonstrated what to Annis
seemed like an almost indecent fertility—trying to conceive
a second child.

Like Rosemary, Annis believed that her life and problems had nothing to do with her sister.

Each sister failed to realize—how could she?—that
competing with her sister affected her own fertility. Because
each denied that she had anything at all in common with
her sister, each failed to understand that they shared the
same desire: they both wanted children. Each had received
the same message from their parents: that having children
was the best thing a woman could do.

Yet each failed to understand that the intense competition between them—now focused on having children—
resulted in Rosemary's producing too many children too
close together and Annis's producing not enough children
too far apart.

Voice is defeated when either of the people "hanging in

there" secretly wants to dominate the other. Although Rosemary and Annis both believed that their blood bond meant they were hanging in for life, neither could use voice actively in their relationship because each was locked into their competition for difference.

Although the older-sister position is the one we usually associate with domination, the relationship between Rosemary and Annis makes it clear that *both* older and younger sister positions can involve the desire to dominate.

Both Rosemary and Annis desired a victory symbolized by their difference. Each wanted to dominate the other's life by the example of her own life events. For Annis, the older sister, domination meant continuing to be the sister who behaved responsibly and well. Annis did things the "right" way. She won their competition when her traditional marriage followed her traditional college career. She won when, despite a deep desire for more children, her babies were "properly" spaced.

At the same time, however, Rosemary also won—by losing. As the younger sister, Rosemary assumed that whatever she did, she was a loser in comparison to her sister. Certainly an unplanned pregnancy, interrupted schooling, and more babies than she could possibly handle confirmed that identification. But, at a deeper level, Rosemary dominated her sister. Without effort, she conceived the babies Annis deeply desired.

And although Rosemary gave up Annis's reward—their parents' approval—she lived in a way that eventually, many years later, permitted her to make real choices about her life.

"When I returned to school after my kids were grown, I finally had enough self-confidence both to study the subjects that interested me and to succeed in my classes,"

Rosemary said. "I know now that it was raising all those children—when my parents were telling me that having them at all confirmed what an idiot I was—that gave me a real sense of self-esteem. Despite what they said, I knew I was doing something right."

Both Rosemary and Annis won their competition. And they both lost.

Even now, although each realizes that years of their lives were absorbed in a competition scripted for them before they were born, each still invests much of herself in being the older or younger sister.

As much as they long to do so, Rosemary and Annis have not given up their desire to dominate each other. Only now, because they also want to be closer to each other, they translate that desire into a wish to *be* dominated. Each sister tries to praise the other by holding up her own life to negative scrutiny.

When friends compete with the secret desire to dominate the result is much the same.

Amanda, thirty-three, and Kendall, thirty-two, think of themselves as very good friends. They have known each other since they were children. However, their "good" friendship is marked by constant irritation for Kendall. "Amanda's part of my life," she said, "I've known her too long not to think we'll always know each other. But I have to admit, most of the time when we go out together I come home feeling like I should put a bag over my head and shoot myself.

"Amanda's major hangup is being attractive to men. No matter where we are or what we're doing, if men are around, she'll talk to them and ignore me. I can take that. I know she's not really in control of herself," said Kendall.

"But what makes me feel awful is when she sets me up to be the 'plain' sister. In other words, in order to feel attractive, she has to make me feel unattractive."

But when I asked Kendall why she put up with Amanda's behavior, she became confused. "I guess I know what Amanda's doing, but somehow, when it's happening, it feels like my fault. It's only when I get home that I get angry. And then we'll talk a couple of days later and I forget my anger. She probably wouldn't even know what I was talking about. And anyway, I guess I *am* less attractive than she is. Maybe I'm just jealous of her."

Despite Kendall's realization that her friendship with Amanda is based on being dominated, Kendall won't confront Amanda. Kendall is a younger sister, well trained in submission, and Amanda, an only child, probably *doesn't* know she dominates Kendall, since she is relating to Kendall in a way established early in their childhoods.

Both Amanda and Kendall have agreed—by keeping it secret—to live with the imbalance of power that *is* their relationship. But Kendall knows what Amanda does not: that they do not have a friendship. They have a feudal relationship, which keeps Kendall Amanda's serf.

The way out *is* very difficult. Finally, though, neither sisters nor friends really want to dominate each other. Instead, they want the sort of relationship that is based on a loving equality, where competition is experienced as a mutual challenge.

## HANGING IN THERE: MUTUALITY AND COMPETITION BETWEEN SISTERS AND FRIENDS

Sisters think they don't use voice because they don't have to. They believe that their blood bond means no exit. However, in their silence they deny themselves the possibility of arriving at genuinely creative ways of resolving their competition. In fact, they deny themselves creativity at all. Instead, they tacitly accept restricted, *uncreative* lives, where each strives to be different from the other by making narrow, limited, and unconscious choices to do and be what her sister is not.

In contrast, as Carol Gilligan's research tells us, the development of adolescent girls hinges on their understanding that competition is a form of disagreement. Girls grow up to the degree to which they recognize that they can disagree with each other *while remaining in connection.* Yet, all too often, sisters remain adolescent with each other exactly because they fail to recognize that their competition is a disagreement, not a battleground from which only one will emerge alive.

When sisters remain embattled for life, both are left for dead.

Real change occurs only when genuine loyalty is present. Change—and growth—is impossible when the only sort of loyalty available permits us to imagine that leaving will solve all our problems. When sisters fail to talk to each other, and when friends leave each other, we insist on no change, neither in ourselves nor in our relationship.

As sisters and friends, we need to revise our perception of noncompetition as morally right. The concept of "voice" implies exactly the reverse.

*Competition* is the moral act. Competition provides the space to "hang in there," facing disagreement, facing another desire, and looking straight at the parts of ourselves we dislike most. Competition means insisting on attachment as the *motive* for change, and insisting that loyalty means that a relationship changes as the people sharing it grow.

Thinking of competition as a moral act allows us to realize that it is a *mutual* act as well. It is only when friends or sisters secretly want to dominate each other, when we secretly base our individual identities on feeling superior to each other, that competition *is* immoral and breeds unethical behavior.

Sometimes, however, recognizing competition means allowing domination to occur. Sometimes attachment and loyalty are demonstrated best by letting the sister or friend win.

The general noncompetition practiced by friends usually encompasses arenas of specific competition. However, good friends know that all competitions are not equal. For example, Peggy, forty-four, and Rene, forty-six, are very good friends. Meeting when both were mothers of young children twenty years ago, they have remained attached to each other through divorce, child rearing, and professional development.

Each admires the other, and each takes enormous pleasure in the other's company, in her humor, her intelligence, and her desire to "be there" for the other. But not in the kitchen.

As Rene tells the story, Peggy nods ruefully, at the same time shaking with laughter. "I realized years ago that the only place there was real tension between us was in the kitchen," said Rene. "We've cooked together so many times over the years, from simply giving the kids lunch to hosting joint dinner parties. Gradually, I understood that being in the kitchen with Peggy was a mixed experience. I love being with her, but when she cooks and cleans up, she's a tiger. Even when we're in my house, she tells me what to do, even how to put the aluminum foil around the leftovers.

"But," continued Rene, "I also realized that I didn't care. It's just not my issue to be very competent in the kitchen. I know I'm as competent as I want to be. But since it's so important to her, I let her have this one. In fact, since I know that the more commands she can give, the better she feels, I usually pretend to be even less competent than I am."

Listening to Rene, Peggy nodded thoughtfully. "I've always believed that I don't compete with my friends. But Rene is right. When I'm in the kitchen I feel exceptionally stressed. I suppose it has to do with my mother, who was an absolutely wonderful cook. She made me feel that whatever I cooked was never quite right. I know very well how competent Rene is. But I guess I have always allowed myself to believe that her abilities fall off in the kitchen. That way, being bossy, I felt like I was taking care of her."

Yet, since Rene and Peggy really are good friends, Rene quickly found a way to explain their kitchen experience as a mutual dynamic.

"You are domineering, but I really don't mind. I feel like *I'm* taking care of *you*, because I know how stressed you get. Giving in doesn't mean I'm giving up," said Rene. "If we interacted that way about everything, our friendship wouldn't work. But we don't. And I'm sure there is an issue that stresses me more than you where you let me be the boss."

"Right," said Peggy, laughing. "Think about how you feel when we talk about books. I'm a big reader, but Rene teaches literature. I know that it's been hard for her to get to the point where she believes that her professional competence is real and not a pretense. So I let her have the authority when we talk about what we're reading. She doesn't cut me off, not at all, but I know she feels better if she has the last word. As she said about being in the kitchen, it's not my issue."

Although Rene and Peggy began our conversation insisting that they did not compete with each other, they realized as they talked that at least part of their relationship is based on a carefully structured competition.

Both Rene and Peggy are oldest sisters. Together, they have developed a mutually acceptable, mutually affirming, balance of power.

Like Rene and Peggy, most of us *do* know when our friends are competing with us. Our finely tuned perception of each other picks up the signals, no matter how subtle they might be, so learning how to make competition mutual is learning how to use those signals in the service of, rather than against, the relationship.

Early in their friendship, Rene and Peggy figured out that they "work well together" because they are both "very competitive," said Peggy.

"We realized," added Rene, "that we each need to be the center of attention sometimes. We don't want to share the center, we want to be it. But we learned that we're both willing to give up being the center. If it's appropriate, either of us will get offstage."

When is it "appropriate" to let a friend or a sister win? According to Rene and Peggy, appropriateness has to do with perception of need.

Real loyalty, for these two friends, means that each is aware of the other's emotional state—aware but not judgmental. Each has decided that their relationship is more important than constant "equality."

"I guess you could say we use each other; we show each other off," Peggy continued. "In general, but especially when we're in a group, we compete to enhance each other, to bring out the other."

Rene and Peggy trust that their competition will not destroy their relationship. In fact, they believe their relationship is strong *because* they compete. They have learned that their competition signals a need for attention. They have learned that their competition means they want attention *from each other*.

"This friendship has taken a lot of work over many years," said Rene. "We compete so well because we trust each other. We trust that each of us will tell the other when feelings get hurt. We trust that neither of us will leave when we disagree."

## AND THEN THEY LIVED HAPPILY EVER AFTER: CHALLENGE AND CONFRONTATION BETWEEN FRIENDS AND SISTERS

Rene and Peggy have learned something else as well. They learned not to be frightened when they sense competition from each other.

For most of us, competition produces fear in two ways. The first is the response we feel to our own competitiveness. The second is our response to our friend's intense emotion, the emotion evoked in her by the issue about which she is competing.

Often, our friend's emotion is a form of high anxiety or stress. It frightens us. Even when the competition is "not our issue," we may be loath to confront our friend.

In part, we are protecting her from herself. We are trying to calm her down without telling her she is responding excessively. But at the same time, we fear that her intense emotional state means that if we confront her, she will leave us, even if we try to "hang in there" with her.

Few of us know ourselves well enough to know all the issues that make us feel exceptionally anxious, that make us seek to dominate other people so that we can divert ourselves from our own unbearable emotion.

Thinking about our family position helps, at least somewhat. Knowing we are older sisters, that we tend to be unduly responsible, that we need to be in authority, that situations where we feel our authority is in question make us anxious, allows us to be more aware of our responses.

Knowing that we are younger sisters, that we tend to submit too easily, that we automatically think we are losing a competition and so become unnecessarily defensive when we are asked to enter one, also helps.

Further, knowing that we are older or younger sisters but that we sometimes feel like the opposite permits us to understand our need to complete ourselves, to replace inside us the sister we left so long ago.

Especially important, though, we need to recognize that when we feel frightened at the notion of competing with our friends, we are really frightened about abandonment. We are afraid our friends—or we—will leave.

Most of the women I interviewed identified, over and over again, the same set of circumstances about which they believed competition with friends was most destructive.

What happened when one of two good friends married, while the other remained single? Or when one friend simply started dating seriously, while the other still sought a romantic relationship?

What happened when one friend became professionally

successful, removing her from her friend's life, either because she moved to a new city or because she moved up the
corporate ladder?

What happened when one friend bought a new outfit the
other friend could not afford? What happened when one
friend lost the five pounds—or ten or twenty—the other
friend still struggled with?

All of these situations can be categorized as competitions
to stay the same.

Each of the women telling her version felt somehow
betrayed by her more successful friend, somehow abandoned, and somehow guilty about envying her friend's success. Each of them also felt even more guilty when *she* was
the successful friend.

All of these scenarios reveal how tenuous women feel
their friendships to be. There is no formal institution, like
marriage or sisterhood, to make friendship valid and permanent. They demonstrate that friendship is about choice,
and they reveal that most women confuse commitment
with similarity.

When our children are disruptive and angry, we don't leave
them. Instead, we try to help them through a difficult time.
When our spouses try our patience, we don't leave them,
either. Even the most conflicted and damaging marriages
can continue long after both partners realize the emptiness
of the relationship.

Yet, as often, we aren't bound to our spouses and children just because we love them. We're bound because we
share an institution with them. They are our family; they
are our "marriage."

Women who are friends do not have an institution to
certify their relationship. Ironically, this lack can mean that

our friendships are more frightening to us than our family relationships. It is in our relationships with our friends that we experience the naked outlines of commitment. It is with our friends that we test our courage to attach.

For example, when I married for the second time I faced disrupting the friendships I had spent the five years between marriages creating. Suddenly, because I was again married, everyone around me, including my friends, seemed to make a tacit assumption that my friendships would wane as I drew closer to my new husband. However, second marriages can correct faulty assumptions made the first time around, just as relationships with friends can correct relationships with sisters.

Now, in my forties, I realized that giving up my friends would also mean damaging my relationship with my husband. Demonstrating disloyalty to my friends would harm my self-esteem.

I knew that being loyal to my new husband meant knowing that I could be loyal at all. And I realized that these were not alternative relationships—they were equally significant. I realized that I was not involved in a competition about affection. I was engaged in a competition for time.

Since I saw more of my husband than my friends, he *seemed* more important than my friends. I knew that I would need to make an explicit commitment to my friends, a commitment in action, not merely words.

Working it out, of course, is not so easy. Commitments are not easy. Often I find that during the evenings I spend with my friends I feel a subliminal guilt about not being with my husband. And when I'm with my husband, I frequently feel equally torn. Since I want to spend time with my two children also, sometimes I feel torn apart, but I am certain that the effort is worthwhile. Identifying the real competition for time has made the other competition—about attachment—vanish.

Now it's easy to celebrate my friends' successes, to affirm them as well as to nurture them, and to be affirmed and nurtured by them. Now it's easy—or at least easier—to disagree with my friends. I am not so afraid, any longer, that if we are different we will leave each other.

I am not so afraid because I have chosen not to leave. I want my friends there in my life for the rest of my life, just as I want my husband and children.

And just as I want my sister. When we commit ourselves to our friends, we also have the chance to commit ourselves to our sisters. We have learned the difference between choice and necessity. We have the chance to choose our sisters as our friends.

In our society, women are taught that confrontation is inevitably angry. We believe that confrontation means conflict, so when we think about confronting our friends or our sisters, we think about fighting with them. But, as Jean Baker Miller writes, cooperation is not always appropriate when we must face our friend's difference, when we must face our own.

We don't need to confront our friends or our sisters with anger, however. Instead, good friends who have decided not to leave each other learn that confrontation can strengthen their relationship.

When we confront each other with anger, we reveal how frightened the confrontation makes us feel, and our fear makes us forget, as well, that we can be different yet attached to each other. Instead, choosing each other, friends and sisters can experience confrontation as a necessary part of the relationship, even a part to be desired rather than avoided.

For example, several years ago I had dinner with one of my closest friends and another woman we both liked, a woman my friend knew, for one reason or another, better than I did.

During dinner, my friend's friend indicated that most of her ideas and opinions were different from mine. Since both of us were fairly secure about who we were, the differences that quickly emerged were acceptable—to us, but not to my friend.

As the evening progressed, I realized that my friend would follow up anything I said with an explanation. I realized that she was trying to protect me from myself. She was trying, because our difference made her so uncomfortable, to erase that difference by erasing my contribution to our discussion.

I also realized that my friend really cared about me. Knowing that, I was able, the next morning, to confront her. Even then, the confrontation wasn't easy. However, it also wasn't angry. With as much calmness as I could muster, I explained that I felt she had silenced me the night before, and that as much as I appreciated her desire to take care of me, I really could take care of myself.

Now, I think we are better friends than we were before. Now each of us appreciates our differences because now we also know that our difference doesn't mean our separation. We defend each other's right to have an opinion, even when it is one we don't hold ourselves. Now, we aren't ashamed of or embarrassed by each other. We have learned that we can look each other in the eye and see the mirror cracked wide open to reveal another person, not our own reflection. Learning how to confront each other, we learned how to disagree. Learning how to disagree, we learned how to choose each other.

While we can learn that calm confrontation generally makes relationships stronger, it's harder to realize that confrontations can be funny. Competition can be fun.

Recently I invited my four closest friends to dinner. By the end of the evening we found ourselves in the kitchen, the place in the house in which most women our age still feel most comfortable. Since things have changed in our society, the men who live with us were in the kitchen too. But the women were at the center of the group.

Two of my friends are big talkers. At a party they blossom when they can entertain. Leaning against the dishwasher, I watched them compete with each other as the talk became more and more excited. They filled the room, each competing, confronting, and challenging the other to go one better, to be more witty, smarter, attractive, perceptive, and stimulating. At one point they even competed for breath.

I realized that they both won. And so did I, so did the men in the room, and so did our fourth friend, who sat, as I did, watching them, convulsed with laughter.

We all won, because finally they were in a competition for happiness. They were using each other to bring out what each admired most about herself. And we, their audience, competed with each other, and with them, to make the best of ourselves—to make ourselves happy.

Well, it was a very good party.

Some stories really do have happy endings. This is one of them, but it doesn't conclude with Cinderella and her prince riding off to their castle in the sky, nor does it confuse happiness with allowing the storyteller to dominate and control the story. This ending doesn't mistake consolation for pleasure, or confuse pleasure with perfection.

Now, thinking about that evening, I realize something—someone—was missing: my sister. I wish she could have been there, among all of us.

But this is a happy ending because it insists on more story.

"Encore, encore!" I wanted to shout when my friends, exhausted, completed their competitive game. I realized that with them I was living the dream of sisterhood, because it was a dream we would have to live over and over again. Sometimes we would get it right, and sometimes we would get it wrong.

But we had chosen to keep on dreaming.

# Bibliography

Atwood, Margaret, *Cat's Eye* (New York: Doubleday, 1989).

Bank, Stephen P., and Michael D. Kahn, *The Sibling Bond* (New York: Basic Books, 1988).

Belenky, Mary Field, Blythe McVicker Clinchy, Nancy Rule Goldberger, and Jill Mattuck Tarule, *Women's Ways of Knowing: The Development of Self, Voice, and Mind* (New York: Basic Books, 1986).

Belkin, Lisa, "Bars to Equality of Sexes Seen as Eroding, Slowly," *New York Times*, August 21, August 22, 1989.

Bellow, Saul, *Humboldt's Gift* (New York: Viking, 1975).

Benjamin, Jessica, *The Bonds of Love: Psychoanalysis, Feminism, and the Problem of Domination* (New York: Pantheon Books, 1988).

Bernay, Toni, and Dorothy W. Cantor, *The Psychology of Today's Woman: New Psychoanalytic Visions* (Cambridge, Mass.: Harvard Univ. Press, 1989).

Bettelheim, Bruno, *The Uses of Enchantment* (New York: Alfred A. Knopf, 1976).

Briles, Judith, *Woman to Woman: From Sabotage to Support* (New Jersey: New Horizons Press, 1987).

Chodorow, Nancy, *Feminism and Psychoanalytic Theory* (New Haven: Yale Univ. Press, 1989).

———, *The Reproduction of Mothering: Psychoanalysis and the Sociology of Gender* (Berkeley: Univ. of California Press, 1978).

Eichenbaum, Luise, and Susie Orbach, *Between Women: Love,*

*Envy, and Competition in Women's Friendships* (London: Penguin Books, 1987).

————, *Understanding Women: A Feminist Psychoanalytic Approach* (New York: Basic Books, 1983).

Eiseley, Loren, *The Immense Journey* (New York: Vintage Books, 1946).

Freud, Sigmund, *Dora: An Analysis of a Case of Hysteria* (New York: Macmillan Books, 1983; original publication: Hogarth Press, 1905).

Friedman, Edwin H., *Friedman's Fables* (New York: Guilford Press, 1990).

————, *Generation to Generation: Family Process in Church and Synagogue* (New York: Guilford Press, 1985).

Fromm, Erich, *The Art of Loving* (New York: Harper & Row, 1956).

————, *Beyond the Chains of Illusion* (New York: Harper & Row, 1962).

————, *The Greatness and Limitation of Freud's Thought* (New York: Harper & Row, 1980).

Gilligan, Carol, *In a Different Voice: Psychological Theory and Women's Development* (Cambridge, Mass.: Harvard Univ. Press, 1982).

————, *Mapping the Moral Domain: A Contribution of Women's Thinking to Psychology, Theory, and Education* (Cambridge, Mass.: Harvard Univ. Press, 1988).

Goffman, Erving, *The Presentation of Self in Everyday Life* (Woodstock, N.Y.: Overlook Press, 1973).

Hirschman, Albert, *Exit, Voice, and Loyalty: Responses to Decline in Firms, Organizations, and States* (Cambridge, Mass.: Harvard Univ. Press, 1970).

Hochschild, Arlie, *The Second Shift* (New York: Viking, 1989).

Horney, Karen, *Feminine Psychology* (New York: W. W. Norton & Co., 1967).

James, William, *The Principles of Psychology*, vol. 1 (New York: Holt, 1890).

Kaplan, Helen Singer, *Disorders of Sexual Desire* (New York: Brunner, Mazel, 1979).

Kolbenschlag, Madonna, *Kiss Sleeping Beauty Goodbye* (New York: Harper & Row, 1988).

LaBier, Douglas, *Modern Madness: The Emotional Fallout of Success* (New York: Addison Wesley, 1986).

Laskas, Jeanne Marie, "When Twins Marry," *Washington Post Magazine*, July 23, 1989.

Le Guin, Ursula, *Dancing at the Edge of the World* (New York: Grove Press, 1989).

Lessing, Doris, *The Four-Gated City* (New York: Alfred A. Knopf, 1969).

———, *Prisons We Choose to Live Inside* (New York: Harper & Row, 1987).

Maccoby, Michael, *The Leader: A New Face for American Management* (New York: Simon & Schuster, 1981).

———, *Why Work?: Leading the New Generation* (New York: Simon & Schuster, 1988).

McGrath, Ellie, *My One and Only: The Special Experience of the Only Child* (New York: Wm. H. Morrow, 1989).

Milk, Leslie, "100 Most Powerful Women," *Washingtonian Magazine*, Sept. 1989, vol. 24, no. 12, pp. 132–135, 200–207.

Miller, Jean Baker, *Psychoanalysis and Women* (London: Penguin Books, 1973).

———, *Toward a New Psychology of Women* (Boston: Beacon Press, 1986).

Miner, Valerie, and Helen E. Longino, *Competition: A Feminist Taboo* (New York: The City Univ. Press, 1987).

Munro, Alice, *The Moons of Jupiter* (New York: Alfred A. Knopf, 1984).

Pearson, Carol, Donna L. Shavlik, and Judith G. Touchton, *Educating the Majority: Women Challenge Tradition in Higher Education* (New York: Macmillan, 1989).

Person, Ethel, *Dreams of Love and Fateful Encounters: The Power of Romantic Passion* (London: Penguin Books, 1988).

Rich, Adrienne, *Of Woman Born: Motherhood as Experience and Institution* (New York: W. W. Norton & Co., 1976).

Sale, Roger, *Fairy Tales and After: From Snow White to E. B. White* (Cambridge, Mass.: Harvard Univ. Press, 1978).

Schaef, Anne Wilson, *Women's Reality: An Emerging Female System in a White Male Society* (New York: Harper & Row, 1981).

Schwartz, Felice, "The 'Mommy Track' Isn't Anti-Woman," *Harvard Business Review*, January–February 1989.

Shreve, Anita, *Remaking Motherhood: How Working Mothers Are Shaping Our Children's Future* (New York: Ballantine Books, 1987).

Sternberg, Robert J., and Michael L. Barnes, *The Psychology of Love* (New Haven: Yale Univ. Press, 1988).

Sessums, Kevin, "The Women Who Still Sleep with the Rolling Stones," *Vanity Fair*, September 1989.

Thomas, Lewis, *The Medusa and the Snail: More Notes of a Biology Watcher* (New York: Viking Press, 1979).

Toman, Walter, *Family Constellations* (New York: Springer, 1969).

Welch, Patrick, "The Cult of the Super-Girl," *Washington Post*, December 18, 1988.

Weldon, Fay, *The Heart of the Country* (New York: Viking, 1989).

————, *Polaris and Other Stories* (London: Penguin Books, 1988).

Wharton, Edith, *Roman Fever and Other Stories* (New York: Scribner, 1911).

Winnicott, D. W., *Collected Papers: Through Paediatrics to Psycho-Analysis* (London: Tavistock, 1958).

————, *The Maturational Processes and the Facilitating Environment* (London: Hogarth Press, 1965).

————, *Playing and Reality* (London: Tavistock, 1971).

# Index